FRANK LLOYD WRIGHT'S STAINED GLASS & LIGHTSCREENS

FRANK LLOYD WRIGHT'S

STAINED GLASS & LIGHTSCREENS

TEXT AND PHOTOGRAPHS
by THOMAS A. HEINZ

Gibbs Smith, Publisher
Salt Lake City

To the memory of Rich Branom, 1933–1999

Over the years many people have been of assistance in this quest for information. They include Paul Crist of Santa Fe Springs, California; Lumbovar Wandzura of Giannini & Hilgart, Chicago; Chicago Metallic Corporation; Michael Fitzsimmons of Chicago; John Toomey of Oak Park; Scott Elliott of St. Joseph, Michigan; Don Kalec and John Thorpe of The Frank Lloyd Home and Studio, Oak Park; Wilbert Hasbrouck of Chicago; Bruce Brooks Pfeiffer of The Frank Lloyd Wright Foundation; David Hanks of New York City; Sharon Darling of Chicago; Mark Henderson of the Getty Center, Los Angeles; Walter and David Judson of The Judson Studios, Los Angeles; Randell L. Makinson of Pasadena; all of the wonderful homeowners who have been so gracious in allowing me access to their beautiful treasures; The National Endowment for two Fellowships that allowed me to travel to see more examples and to visit several archives for information. Generous thanks to my family and to Ann T. Heinz for her patience and insights.

First Paperback Edition
10 09 08 07 06 05   5 4 3 2 1

Text © 2000 Thomas A. Heinz
Photographs © 2000 Thomas A. Heinz unless otherwise noted

Published by
Gibbs Smith, Publisher
P. O. Box 667
Layton, Utah 84041

Orders: (1-800) 748-5439
Website: *www.gibbs-smith.com*

Cover design by O'Very Covey
Interior design and production by Steven R. Jerman—Jerman Design Incorporated, Salt Lake City, Utah
Printed and bound in China

Library of Congress Cataloging-in-Publication Data

Heinz, Thomas A.
    Frank Lloyd Wright's stained glass and lightscreens / by Thomas A. Heinz.— 1st ed.
        p. cm.
    Includes index.
    ISBN 0-87905-610-X (hb); 1-58685-843-2 (pbk)
    1. Wright, Frank Lloyd, 1867–1959. 2. Glass art—United States.
    3.Glass painting and staining—United States. I. Title.

    NK5398.W78 H46 2000
    748.5913—dc21

                                                                00-021370

Contents

Preface

Glass, and especially art glass, has interested me as long as I can remember. During high school and college, I saw beautiful blown pieces at the art fairs and several of Wright's windows at the Art Institute of Chicago.

When I first saw the Wright houses in person, it was the lightscreens that held my attention, more than any other detail or design. The intricate, ordered patterns and the craftsmanship amazed me when I tried to re-create them from memory, and after taking an evening course in stained glass construction, I understood the work on a different plane.

I began to research Wright's glass after graduating from the University of Illinois, Urbana, in architecture. While working at the Illinois Central Railroad, I had several projects working on old buildings and restoring several large art-glass windows, mosaics, and terrazzo installations. Learning that Giannini & Hilgart was still in business, I began making a long series of lunchtime visits to their studio looking for information. This led to an informal course apprenticing to the owner, who had been trained by Mr. Hilgart. He taught me how to build a window, and I made several that were installed in commercial locations in Chicago. While in his studio, I studied some old doors that were stored there, and found some old cartoons or drawings, then located some of the houses to study the executions of those drawings.

I had offered findings of my firsthand research to David Hanks for his book on Wright's decorative arts and to the Chicago Historical Society for their exhibit on Chicago's glass and ceramics. These led to receiving two grants from the National Endowment to study residential art glass in the U.S., and I traveled to see what had been done in cities outside of Chicago, mostly in the East.

In Los Angeles I came upon Paul Crist, an expert in the glass and lampshades of Tiffany. Together we researched Wright's glass and found glass chemists and glassmakers in a small studio near Fallingwater. We were able to exactly re-create the color, texture, and seeds found in the original glass used in the Martin House and the Dana House. Through finding the materials and re-creating the process of iridizing this glass, we learned that the process causes a major problem: the color of the base glass changes when re-fired. Having access to the original lamps at the Dana House before purchase by the State of Illinois, and before the original patina was removed by locals working at the house, we were able to reproduce the lamps so closely that a serious antiques collector with a good eye for detail and fakery had a difficult time distinguishing between the original and our copy.

Having personally visited every Wright building, I have studied every window and installation that is known to exist and have also found many that have been removed from their original buildings. I have examined those limited number of drawings that exist at the Frank Lloyd Wright archives at Taliesin and have gone through all the correspondence I could locate on Wright's windows. Surprisingly, there is very little. My two previous books on Wright's stained glass are the only two on the subject.

All this is to explain the nature of the original research that supports the claims and paths of logic that lead to assumptions and conclusions in this writing. These unique designs are very difficult to describe in words. I hope that my photographs help perpetuate an understanding of Wright's lightscreen creations and lead to further research and discovery.

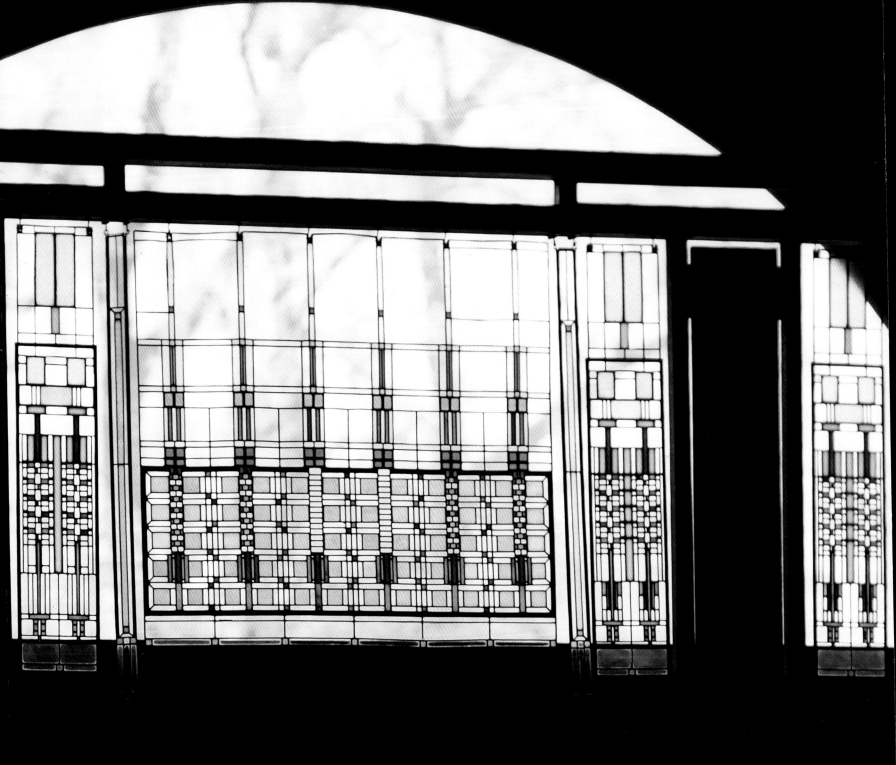

Introduction

"Glass and light—two forms of the same thing!"

—Frank Lloyd Wright, *Architectural Record,* July 1928

In thirty years of study of Frank Lloyd Wright's designs, it has become ever more clear to this author that Wright was a genius in his treatment of light. He was apparently intrigued with its properties, with shadow and pattern created by light as it entered the home environment.

Over his career, Wright wrote very little about his own buildings. He left a legacy of philosophical writings and critical essays, but insight into his own designs is skimpy, to say the least. Necessarily, then, in any study of Wright's work, a scholar or author must make some assumptions or draw conclusions based on physical evidence, on others' writings about Wright as a man and as an architect, and on chronological development of Wright's designs over the decades.

In the couple of articles that do exist, Wright used the term "lightscreens" (spelled variously as an open word and closed) when referring to something that would modify the pattern or view of light in an opening, whether the opening be an outside wall, inside wall, or ceiling. So this seems an appropriate term for us to use when talking about his specialized treatments for windows, lighting, and screens. This study does not limit our view to only his colored leaded glasswork, but opens our perspective to his manipulations of light and pattern in a variety of ways. It is clear that Wright considered light to be a major design element.

Hanging art-glass screen, Studio, Susan Lawrence Dana House, 1904, Springfield, Illinois. Most of Frank Lloyd Wright's designs for lightscreens were for windows where the materials had to keep out the rain and wind. This screen, hanging in space about a foot from the window, is perhaps the purest form of a Wright lightscreen, since its only purpose is artistic. Nine panels of several sizes are suspended from a wood frame protected from the elements by a half circle of clear plate glass. The pattern is abstract and does not appear to be a representation of any plant or other life form, as are most of Wright's other works. This photograph was taken before the remodeling of the house. Notice the difference between the patterns at the bottom of the medium-sized panels on either side of the wood columns; the right set has additional elements when compared to the left set. The earliest photographs show the panels set in a symmetrical series. Zinc cames missing from parts of the left side of the central panel were restored during a later remodeling.

1

Luxfer prisms, 1897.

Early in his career (1900, when Wright was thirty years old and would have been a relative upstart), Wright's genius for light treatments was acknowledged in a *Brush and Pencil* magazine article by Harry D. Kirk on modern styles. Though his work wasn't discussed in the article, at least two of Wright's designs were shown—one for the Luxfer Prism Company and one from the Chauncey Williams House (1897)—along with those of Tiffany and LaFarge. There is no question that Kirk intended to position Wright in the same class as these well-established luminaries of stained-glass design.

In a phrase, Wright became the equivalent of Tiffany but in a geometric sense. Whereas Tiffany was doing representational designs, Wright was doing abstractions. Glass designs by both these men are still highly sought today and are copied for popular uses ad infinitum.

Before we delve into the specifics of Wright's work, we need to establish a context for glass and its uses.

Development of Windows

Historically, when windows first appeared, they were just holes in the wall. The first improvement was to add a drape to keep out the wind and to hold in the heat. When clear sheet glass was developed around A.D. 1000, window design moved ahead. These sheets of glass were developed from a blown-glass vessel. A large, round, vertical-sided vessel, not unlike a glass water bottle for a modern water cooler, was blown. While it was still pliable, the cylinder was cut from the vessel and laid out flat to form a sheet. This method is still being used today for special colors and effects.

Almost as soon as these sheets were developed, designs and patterns came along with them, reflecting the raw materials, times, and culture of their regions.

The materials used to hold glass panes together varied widely, but after the first thousand years of use, there were three that seemed most suitable for windows: lead, wood, and cement. Lead could be easily hand-formed to any thickness and profile using simple tools. Lead was also pliable enough to maintain a weather seal and keep out the rainwater. Sometimes smaller panels of leaded glass were set into larger wood frames to span large window openings.

Wood, while inexpensive and widely available, was best suited to straight lines. Since it is not pliable, wood requires another pliable material to be used in concert to prevent leaking. Wood was used for most residential installations and for smaller formal-style commercial and government buildings. A drawback to wood is that it deteriorates in a relatively short time, as compared to lead and cement, if not properly maintained.

Stone and its man-made equivalent, concrete, can be crafted into any shape, including curves and circles. It does not deteriorate quickly but, like wood, also needs a sealant. This material was used in the largest buildings; Gothic cathedrals come to mind immediately. Their beautiful stone tracery appears to be quite delicate, but the scale of the cathedral must be taken into account. It is quite large and is structurally stable. Nowadays, mostly concrete and epoxy are used for religious installations.

Glass, in many regards, has changed very little over time. Windowpane glass has remained the most consistent in thickness, though the flatness and the clarity have continuously improved over time. Colored glass during the medieval period was available in a small range of colors; blues, reds, and yellows were the most common, and they could be intense. These came in chunks, not large sheets, that had to be pieced together to form designs.

Pindars House, London, circa 1600, Victoria & Albert Museum. This pattern appears to be an elaborate version of a pattern Wright developed for the dining room of the Blossom House, built in 1893 (see p. 39). However, this one continues the texture of the carved-wood panels onto the flat and curved glazed panels. The came is lead. This piece was relocated to the Victoria & Albert Museum in 1890 when the Pindars House was demolished to make room for the Liverpool Street Station expansion.

3

Stained and Art Glass

The term *stained glass* commonly refers to a wide range of styles and materials. It includes colored, enameled, or painted glass. Staining sometimes refers to the color or the stain of the glass itself but is more accurately the painting of a material that is then fired onto the glass surface. Because early glass had a limited palette, painting became a method for creating figures and expanding the range of colors. The subjects of the earliest glass windows, as with the earliest art, were religious. It was not until much later, the thirteenth century, that an ambition to copy nature began to influence artists.

Art glass is a more encompassing term and refers to any artistic fashioning of glass in any form—including beveling, chipping, and sandblasting—to give an artistic effect. These latter forms were often used for commercial purposes such as office doors and advertising signs. The Pullman Palace Car Company of Pullman, Illinois, just south of Chicago, made art glass even more popular in the late 1800s and a sign of luxury, though it was affordable at many scales. The inclusion of many nonreligious installations in the Columbian Exhibition of 1893 also helped to popularize it at a time when Wright was just starting his architectural career. These influences played a part in his choice to include it in many of his earliest buildings, probably due to the encouragement of his clients.

The patterns used in the glass before 1900 were simple borders, French flourishes, or garlands. Landscape windows came along very late. As graphic design developed, there were influences of Art Nouveau and finally the simple, straight lines of the Prairie School led by Wright.

Rarely were any of these stained- or art-glass windows signed by their makers or designers. Because clients could request anything they wanted, designs were not unique to a designer or an art-glass firm in the way that the design of a building was uniquely attributable to an architect of the same period.

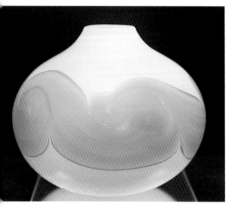

Late-twentieth-century vessel, Chicago. This photograph, taken in daylight, attests that reflected and transmitted light bring out the luminosity of this material.

Each brush stroke in this stained-glass flower detail can be seen in the window, which was located in a church in Quincy, Illinois, that has since burned down.

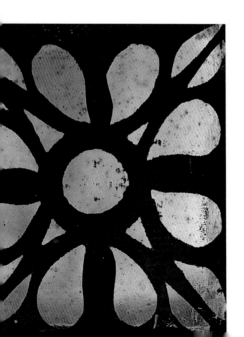

Images in Glass

Everything looks good in glass. This is a result of light hitting the color of the glass and giving it life. Light changes in wavelength as it passes through glass, like a prism. As with other waves, like those in water, when two sets of waves of certain frequencies are next to each other, the colors can blend harmoniously. This is the case with stained glass. Even though segments are separated by the metal—called "came"—that holds the pieces of glass together in a composition, the colored panes appear to be next to each other because light bends around the opaque lines.

Wright's glass designs add a fourth dimension: changes in time. Photographs, unfortunately, only freeze the view. Each day and throughout each day, the changing light alters the appearance of the window. With as much clear glass as Wright often used, the strong and soft light were part of his designs, and the patterns, defined by the clear glass, that drift across the interiors throughout each day add to the special nature of his work.

Art- or stained-glass windows were intended to tell a story in the old cathedrals. Wright, too, intended a story to be told. The clients and their interests are reflected in the patterns and materials used. This echo of the client might be as simple as a favorite color or an initial worked into the window or as elaborate as a depiction of a favorite plant.

Lightscreens

Perhaps the purest example of Wright's designed lightscreen is found in the studio of the Susan Lawrence Dana House in Springfield, built about 1904 (see facing p. 1). Here Wright designed a series of nine sections that hang from a wood frame inside a half-round plate-glass window. The design is purely ornamental and one of the few in the Dana House that are completely abstract. This composition acts as a hanging screen in a location that might otherwise accept a hanging tapestry, but a tapestry would block the light.

Unity Temple gives another prime example. The upper windows of the assembly room, or temple, just inside the massive concrete columns and running across the full width of all four sides, are a continuous sheet of glass. There are no wood frames to interrupt the flow. The windows open as pivots at several points along the length. This, too, is a lightscreen.

Right: Upper window in temple room, Unity Temple, 1906, Oak Park, Illinois.

Below: The upper windows in Unity Temple consist of a series of pivoting windows. These differ from normal windows in that they have no wood frames and are continuous across the entire length of the hall. Many have stated earlier that these windows do not open because they could not see the wood frames that were believed to hold each sash. Wright was very clever here in disguising the functionality of these windows, using the came as the structural frames. The design is intended to soften the junction between the plane of the ceiling and the transparent, perpendicular windows. A dense series of squares interspersed with rectangles of opalescent glass adorns the top of the window panel, with less detail toward the bottom.

When Wright ceased the use of metal and colored glass, he continued to add pattern to the light in the form of a screen. Specific examples are the patterning for the sixteen-inch concrete blocks that formed screens in the John Storer House in Los Angeles (1924) and others of his Los Angeles concrete-block houses of the 1920s.

Facing and below: Concrete screen, John Storer House, 1924, Los Angeles, California.

Wright was always one to get the most out of building materials, and the dry-packed concrete used for these sixteen-inch-square blocks is no exception. Rather than having a plain, flat surface, Wright made the blocks interesting and exciting. The aluminum molds add a very detailed pattern to the face and, where appropriate, perforate the block. These openings let the gentle California breezes flow through the rooms and allow for a certain limited vision through them as well.

The openings were not glazed, but on the interior of the room a glazed sash is set into tracks and acts as a sliding window. This arrangement keeps the outside face clean and allows for various amounts of air to enter the room. Each light is sized to the dimensions of the block, and the muntins are aligned with its joints.

Some blocks Wright laminated with clear plate glass; others he backed with sixteen-inch-wide casement windows. Both examples can be seen in the Alice Millard House of Pasadena.

Never abandoning a good idea, Wright continued to use the lightscreen up to his final design of the 1950s and in nearly all that came before it. There were fanciful cutouts in wood panels or windows in almost all of his houses, completing the cycle begun with the cut wood used in his own house sixty years earlier.

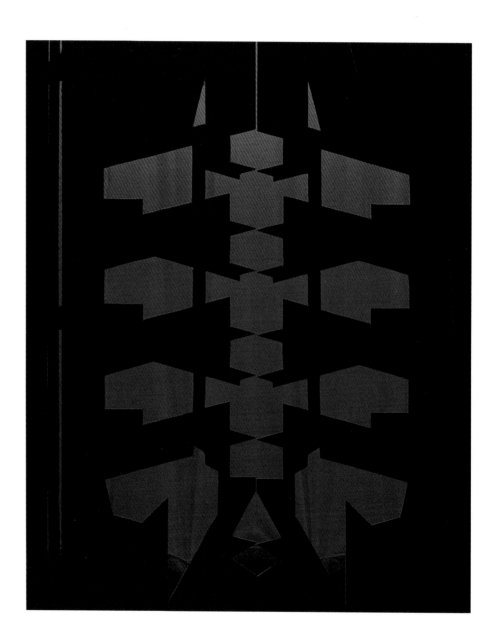

Wood screen (circa 1950), Hillside Building, Taliesin, Spring Green, Wisconsin. There is no glass in this screen. It is a purely decorative element used to define the different spaces on each side of it. The overall pattern is split at the center, and each panel functions as a casement window, pivoting at the sides to swing in and out. Red fabric drapes are the background for the screen, giving a rather dramatic effect.

Making a Modern Art-Glass Window

So that the reader may gain a stronger appreciation for the art-glass designs of Frank Lloyd Wright, a review of the traditional method of creating a window may be enlightening. There are seven steps in creating an art-glass window.

First, create a design. This is usually drawn on paper and indicates the final colors and includes a sketch of any details.

Second, make a full-size pattern with two duplicate copies. This is customarily accomplished by using carbon paper between two paper layers added beneath the art.

Third, cut the second layer into individual shapes using special scissors with two outside blades opposing a third between them. These cut out a thin strip that should be equal to the thickness of the metal came (usually lead) that will take its position between the pieces of glass.

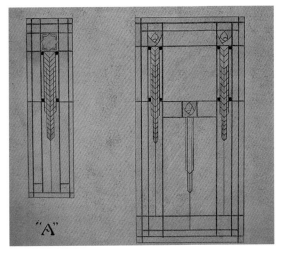

"Roycroft" (left) and Herringbone paper designs, Giannini & Hilgart. The design and size of each window is planned ahead of time, usually by the glassmaker, in this case the Giannini & Hilgart firm. There is no identification or date on these designs, drawn in color on stiff paper.

Giannini & Hilgart, Chicago. Paper pattern and cut glass. Each paper pattern is used to make a precise cut for each piece of glass. The pieces are then placed on the table in the proper position, atop the third and final carbon.

Fourth, place the individual paper shapes on top of the glass, then cut to the precise shape of the pattern.

Fifth, reassemble all the pieces on a flat table according to the original full-size drawing and check for accuracy of fit and consistency.

Sixth, assemble the metal that binds the glass in place. Pieces of the metal must be measured and calculations made for the least amount of waste while providing the greatest strength. At this point, the metal is cut and soldered.

Finally, turn the piece onto its other side and solder the joints and seal with glazing; the piece is complete.

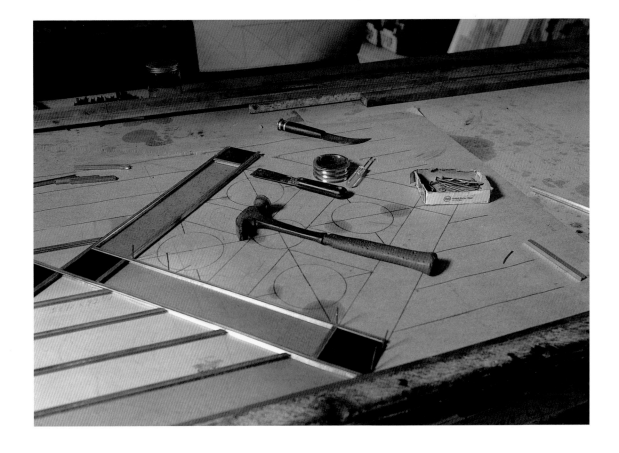

There are several critical points that can make or break a fine piece of art glass. If the cuts

are just a sixteenth of an inch too large, for instance, and if there are as few as sixteen pieces across,

the piece would be a full inch too large. Each piece needs to be cut very accurately. Another factor

is that curves are difficult to cut; there are three pieces of material that must define the same curve:

two pieces of glass, one on each side of the curve, and metal between that also must match the curve.

Curves are complicated. Straight lines are much easier.

It is traditional that each piece of glass be bound by metal on all sides. This would certainly

be the case where the window was installed to keep out the weather. Where it is used as a skylight or

interior window, it would not have to be constrained by these rules of standard procedure.

Glass bins and glazing benches. Wood bins (to the right) in the Giannini & Hilgart glass-making shop, Chicago, contain the supply of glass available for the artisans. On the left, at the window, a rack holds samples of each type of glass and identifies their bin numbers. Paper cutouts for a glass pattern are laid out on the glazing table in the foreground.

Wright worked outside of the envelope, to use a modern phrase. He abandoned the traditional. In one instance at the Willits House, he used glass cut to form a herringbone pattern. To maintain, in proportion, a thin line, there is no metal between the pieces of glass; they hold together by compression. At the other end of the spectrum, in the hanging light of the Little House master bedroom, he set a pattern with the metal but did not include any glass.

The total impact of Wright's lightscreens relied not only on patterns in panes of glass but also the window sashes, jambs, and casing acting like a triple matte on a work of art. In this author's opinion, his genius is weakened, loses some impact in those screens that contain no glass. But where all the elements are working together, this man's art has an overwhelming impact.

Frank Lloyd Wright's Design Development

While many artists work along a single line of development, with each successive piece showing an improvement or other modification, Wright was able to follow several lines simultaneously. At times there were three or four different developments in progress. For the most part, and largely due to budget limitations, there would be a single thematic pattern for any given building. Sometimes, though, as in the Boynton House and even with a limited budget, Wright used several apparently unrelated designs within a single building. Why, one way or the other, is not entirely clear.

The simultaneity presents a problem. How can one tell what is developing and what is successful? If most artists follow a single line, why would Wright follow so many? To answer the second question first, Wright had several very talented collaborators. These included people in his own office, outside designers, and craftsmen who made the pieces. His collaborators were a powerful influence; they were the first line of inspiration. Perhaps the strongest voices, however, were his clients'. They were the last word on what would be put into their houses. Wright's greatest work could be vetoed by a client and would never see the light of day, for the client controlled the purse strings. Unfortunately, there is little documentation of these incidents; the Francis Little House of Minnesota is the best example, but clients having the final say is a natural extension of the client/architect relationship.

The designs presented in this study are not ordered according to the dates of construction. They are arranged by line of development, although even this organization is subject to some authorial discretion. There seem to be two basic lines: one is pattern or design, and the other is materials advances. Some of the designs could appear in more than one section.

Wright's glassworks seem to be the most popular pieces at Wright exhibitions, and reproductions, good and bad, sell well in all arenas. Wright wrote little about his thoughts and ideas on the subject of his art glass. This book will show the many lines of development and many of the best examples created throughout his career. They are shown, as much as possible, in their original context in an effort to re-create Wright's intended impression.

CHAPTER 1

Before Wright

One of the earliest glass patterns to appear in the U.S. that could be considered a style or in common use was the colored border. The pattern consisted of a square or rectangular alignment of brightly colored glass pieces around a nearly square center panel of clear glass. The colors used in the borders were usually blue, red, and yellow, though there appears to be no particular logic to their sequential arrangement. Colored glass was more expensive and rarer than clear glass and thus had to be used sparingly for home construction. The border pattern would often be found only in the front door or in the main window of the living room.

The painting and staining used in many religious windows was not generally found in residential work. The use of individual pieces of glass to construct a pattern is a factor that would differentiate between religious and residential designs.

Hollyhocks, Jenks House, John LaFarge, architect, 1881, Baltimore, Maryland. The bordered designs of the nineteenth century were handled straightforwardly by LaFarge. In use are some of the specialty glasses he developed for his designs. The bracing bar toward the bottom of the center panel splits some of the glass and might be seen as a visual intrusion on the pattern. (Photo © Christie's, New York)

Two stained-glass windows typical of the Victorian period, Victoria & Albert Museum, London.

Chicago as a Center for Stained Glass

Perhaps it was because of its rapid expansion as an industrial center or because of the building required after the great fire of 1871, but Chicago was the center of the art-glass movement. The May 1882 volume of the *Inland Architect* reported,

> *The use of stained glass, for so many centuries confined to the decoration of churches and palaces, has become so universal, that scarcely a house of any architectural pretensions can be found that has not stained glass in door or window, and even to fire screens its use is applied, and here, as every where that the effect of light is available, its beauty is enhanced.*

William Watts Sherman House, 1874, Newport, Rhode Island, Henry Hobson Richardson, architect. The suns and sunflowers depicted in these panes promote a theme popular at the time, espousing the healthful quality of sunlight.

American Architects Using Colored Glass

Henry Hobson Richardson

The greatest architect of the nineteenth century, Henry Hobson Richardson, was able to use painted and stained glass successfully in residential design work. The William Watts Sherman House of Newport, Rhode Island (1874), has a series of yellow suns painted in a second-floor east-facing window. On bright but overcast days, the light entering the hall appears as if it were sunlight. The upper hall lit by this window is always cheerful. On the other hand, Richardson's most famous religious building, Boston's Trinity Church, uses individual pieces of glass in its entrance doors. The patterns are fanciful geometric arrangements much like those found in Owen Jones's *Grammar of Ornament* (1856).

*Looking at a detail of the William Watts Sherman House it is easy to see
that the colors were painted onto the glass.*

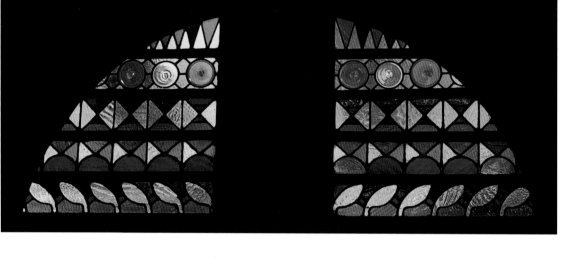

Silsbee & Sullivan

Wright's two employers, Joseph Lyman Silsbee and Adler & Sullivan, used art glass in similar fashions. Both used colored-glass pieces to define their patterns, and neither used painting or staining. Silsbee did not develop a strong decorative style as Sullivan did, but kept most of his vision windows clear, in a wood sash, and confined the art glass to special locations such as round and stairway windows. His patterns were plainer than most classical buildings by other architects of the 1880s and 1890s.

Sullivan developed a unique and distinctive decorative system. His designs were based on the growth of the seedpod, or cotyledon, represented as winged seeds of the maple tree. This representation would be at the growth center of the design but not necessarily the geometric center. From this original, growth would develop in the form of leaves, most often white-oak leaves. These patterns spiraled in several directions in an energetic effusion. Contrary to his own tenet "form follows function," Sullivan's ornament was not designed specific to materials that would represent it; similar patterns can be found in cast iron, terra-cotta, and wood, as well as glass. Because of the complexity of art-glass construction, the cames interrupted the flowing leaves and interfered with the patterns as designed. But the colors used by Sullivan were in keeping with the color schemes of his buildings and were effective in that regard.

20

Right: Merchants Bank of Winona, Purcell & Elmslie, 1911, Winona, Minnesota. The medallion at the center of this large window is typical of the drafting style that was applied to designs for windows by Sullivan and many others of the Prairie School practitioners who surrounded Wright and followed his lead.

Below: Laylight installed in 1889, Auditorium Building, 1886, Chicago, Illinois, Adler & Sullivan, architects.

Clockwise from upper left: Terra-cotta ornament, Wainwright Building, 1890, St. Louis, Missouri. Sullivan & Adler, architects. Cast-iron ornament, Carson Pirie Scott, 1899. Terra-cotta ornament and window, Merchants National Bank, 1913, Grinnell, Iowa, Louis H. Sullivan, architect. Art-glass window, Merchants National Bank, 1913, Grinnell, Iowa. Louis H. Sullivan, architect.

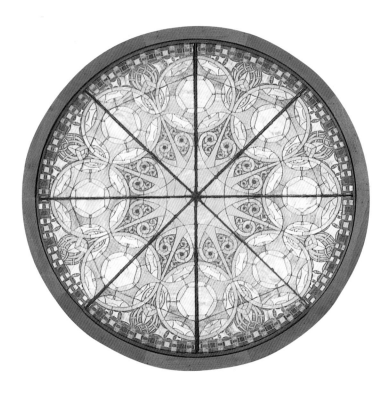

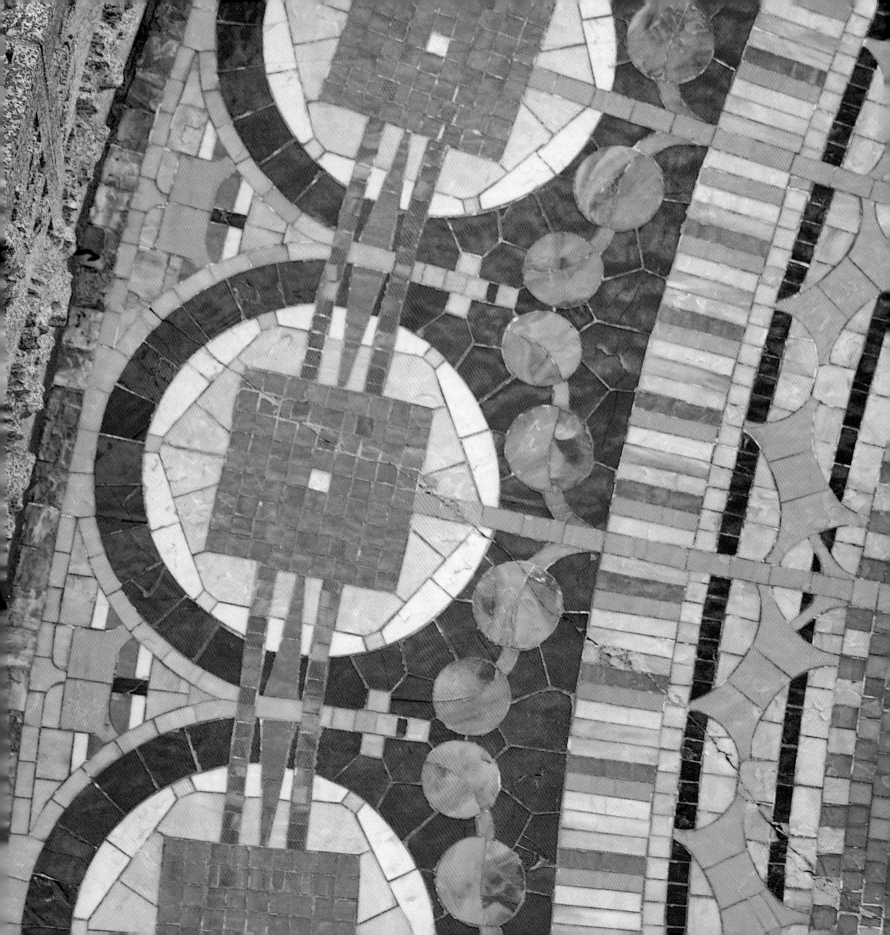

Prairie Architects Maher, Purcell & Elmslie, Drummond, and Van Bergen

Many of Wright's contemporaries ventured into areas as unexplored as did Wright. Robert Spencer, George Washington Maher, Purcell & Elmslie, William Drummond, and John Van Bergen all contributed to the regional abstraction advocated but not illustrated by Sullivan and earlier in the Arts & Crafts movement by William Morris, John Ruskin, and Viollet le Duc.

Overseas architects would have been less influential because Wright would not have been able to see their work in person and discuss it with the creators. There was much going on in Chicago and Wright was busy with his clients; therefore, his ideas developed more as a result of local influences than foreign ones. Because Wright was in contact with the architects working in his region of the country, they would have been a very strong influence on his art-glass designs.

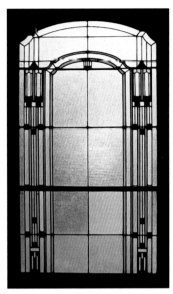

Lightscreen, Blinn House, 1906, Pasadena, California, George W. Maher, architect. This is one of many variations of a Prairie School design on a house that was a long way from the prairie.

Art-glass window installed in 1920, Heidbreder House, circa 1915, Quincy, Illinois, George Behrensmeyer, architect. A typical residential window design of the early twentieth century.

Opposite: Farmers & Merchants Bank, 1919, Columbus, Wisconsin, Louis H. Sullivan. This is one of the many mosaics that Sullivan, Wright's mentor, used throughout his career.

Glass Designers and Manufacturers

Tiffany & LaFarge

In the 1870s, John LaFarge introduced the practice of making pictorial windows in Philadelphia. He had glass folded and textured to represent ground, drapery, foliage, and skies.

Probably the best-known designer and maker of residential art glass, the one who made art glass popular in the late nineteenth and early twentieth century, was Louis Comfort Tiffany (1848–1933). He developed his greatest work at the same time as Wright. Tiffany understood the opportunities of using individual pieces to make the design. He also developed his own types of glass to be used in specific parts of glass he was designing. Tiffany expanded his business and became expert at designing glass for various representations, such as drapery glass for dresses and robes; this glass had variable thickness like the folds in fabric. He also developed glass with the texture of feathers on the surface for creating angels. Another technique Tiffany employed very successfully was that of flashed glass: he sandblasted away the center of a piece of glass having an opalescent base, thus leaving a glow-ing face and creating a three-dimensional effect.

Tiffany was not just innovative with the glass; he also had to invent an artistic method to hold the pieces together. While he was not necessarily the inventor of the copper-foil system, he cer-tainly is the one who put it to the highest and best use. The copper-foil method was more evident in the manufacturing of his beautiful lamp shades than in his windows. The technique involved wrap-ping each piece of glass with a thin ribbon of copper foil that was much like aluminum foil. Presumably, the accurate cut of the glass pieces made for a tight fit. Once the pieces were assembled, they were soldered together. The thickness of the joint could be varied, as could the texture. Additional shapes could be soldered on the top as well as the bottom and over the surface of the glass.

Probably the most amazing thing about the work of the Tiffany Studios was that Louis Comfort Tiffany was able to transfer his artistic vision, as well as his attention to detail, to workers and employees without dilution. The consistency of their output is remarkable.

Pond-lily lampshade, Tiffany Studios #1490-18, circa 1910. The water glass used in this shade is a fine example of the specific glass that was made for just these instances. A wide range of glasses were manufactured by Tiffany, probably the most produced by a glass manufacturer. The water glass helps to give a 3-D effect. This shade was manufactured using the copper-foil method. (Photo © Christie's, New York)

Belcher Mosaic

Others were being equally as innovative as Tiffany but were perhaps not as successful nor as well known. Some of these innovators were addressing different aspects than others. One such was Henry Belcher, who saw an opportunity to make the glass pieces smaller and yet not compromise the strength. His idea was to make the patterns in the mosaic fashion using very small pieces, about one-half inch across. The assembly process used copper foil, and he added metal to it. It is unclear whether this metal was added in a molten state, which would possibly crack the glass, or in an electro process. Many of these windows remain in their original installations and many more have been removed and are in circulation. However, none of these are signed or identified with a label.

Belcher window, circa 1870, collection of Paul Crist, Rancho Santa Fe, California. The small pieces of glass are held in place by a method that borrows from both Tiffany's copper-foil technique and the electroglazing used later in the Luxfer prism installations.

Above and right: Front doors, Gamble House, 1907, Pasadena, California, Greene & Greene, architects. The Gamble House front door is an extension of the copper-foil technique used by Tiffany on his lamp shades. Lead overlapped the glass and additional solder was dripped onto it, giving a rough texture much like the bark of the California live oak figured in the doors. The variable widths of the came give a powerful effect, as does the detail of the small-scale texture of the soldering.

Chicago Metallic Corporation

Chicago Metallic Corporation, begun in 1893, initiated a new process for manufacturing the metal used in art-glass windows. Three Jahn brothers developed a technique that allowed thin, wide ribbons of metals to be run through a series of dies to form a stronger and lighter came. These metals included brass, copper, and zinc. Initially, the shapes mirrored those produced in lead, commonly referred to as an **H** shape. The new aspect that they brought out was named "colonial came." The basic shape looked like two arrowheads on the ends of a short shaft. This added depth as well as great strength to the came. With the stiffer metals, there was little need for support bars within the average window. Chicago Metallic produced twenty styles of came and continues the process today, using the original machines and some of the original dies. When art glass lost favor in the 1940s and '50s, Chicago Metallic used the same die process to introduce what is now known as the suspended ceiling system. The metal **T** was also formed by pulling sheets of metal through dies; Chicago Metallic is one of the largest producers of these metal **T** systems, though it never produced lead came.

Whether Wright knew of Chicago Metallic before he invented his designs is unclear. He may have identified a need for the process, then worked with Chicago Metallic to develop it. Or it is possible that Wright was introduced to Chicago Metallic through his association with client William Winslow and decided to try their products. Winslow and his brother ran the Winslow Brothers Iron Works not far from the Chicago Metallic location but Winslow was also a tinkerer and inventor. It was Winslow's invention that made it possible to form the Luxfer Prism Company. (A fuller discussion of this company follows on page 50.)

Cames and lead. The two cames on the right are lead and those on the left are zinc. The lead is an extruded product. Zinc is manufactured in sheets and folded, as can be seen in this sample manufactured by the Chicago Metallic Corporation.

Kokomo Opalescent Glass Company

Most of Wright's glass can be traced back to the Kokomo Opalescent Glass Company located in north-central Kokomo, Indiana, which began making glass in 1888. All of the art-glass studios that had contracts for Wright's buildings used this glass in some or all of their windows and other products. The face texture and the tiny air bubbles within the sheet of glass, called seeds, are particular to Kokomo. Some Kokomo pieces, specifically for the Martin and Dana Houses, have been traced to particular rollers. For the most part, the iridescence was added by the art-glass manufacturing studios, but in this case it may have been produced as iridescent glass by Kokomo, although they seem to have produced little of it. Kokomo glass was also used by the Tiffany Studios, as evidenced in the glass company's files. Kokomo continues operation and provides glass for many restorations of Wright's buildings.

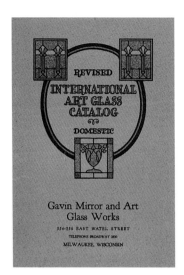

Above and facing: Revised International Art Glass Catalog: Domestic, 50 pages, National Ornamental Glass Manufacturers Association, 1924.

The National Ornamental Glass Association Catalog

In the late nineteenth century, several management and labor groups were formed in Chicago as part of a societal response to urbanization; people were living closer together and desired to join for their own good and improvement. These included the National Ornamental Glass Manufacturers Association of the United States and Canada. They issued two catalogs in 1904 that remained unchanged into the 1930s. These catalogs were often overprinted with the identification of individual art-glass shops and studios and were given to clients to assist in determining a design, to show approximate costs and some of the variations to the cost factors.

There were over 350 different patterns for windows, many in color. The patterns could be ordered as shown for the price given or with alterations in color, figure, and proportion with the price to be negotiated. The glass could be beveled, clear, colored, or opalescent. The came was available in standard lead, in copper or brass plate, or in solid copper. Purchasing multiple units of the same design lowered the unit price.

National Ornamental Glass catalogs introduced the use of standard patterns rather than those designed by architects. In houses not designed by architects, there could be a high-quality design used. This was certainly the case throughout Chicago and the surrounding area. There are rows and rows of speculative housing developments, often referred to as Chicago bungalows, containing these windows. Few of the designs are repeated, however, for seemingly endless variations were requested by the builders.

All of this set the stage for Wright to enter the scene and elevate the art of art glass to new heights.

LEADED CLEAR with COLORED DECORATION
Rules for ordering and further description see general information page

5146. $2.00 sq. ft.   5147. $2.10 sq. ft.   5148. $2.20 sq. ft.   5149. $2.20 sq. ft.

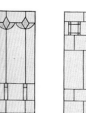
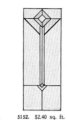
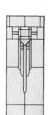
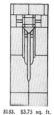

5150. $2.40 sq. ft   5151. $2.50 sq. ft.   5152. $2.40 sq. ft.   5153. $3.75 sq. ft.

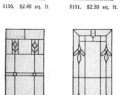
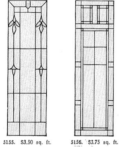
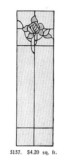

5154. $3.20 sq. ft.   5155. $3.50 sq. ft.   5156. $3.75 sq. ft.   5157. $4.20 sq. ft.

LEADED COLORED GLASS
Rules for ordering and further description see general information page

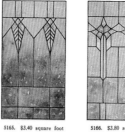

5165. $3.40 square foot   5166. $3.80 square foot   5167. $4.00 square foot

5168. $3.30 square foot   5169. $3.00 square foot   5170. $3.00 square foot

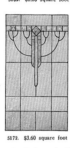

5171. $3.30 square foot   5172. $3.60 square foot   5173. $3.75 square foot

LEADED COLORED GLASS
Rules for ordering and further description see general information page

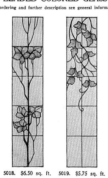

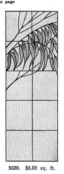

5017. $5.80 sq. ft.   5018. $6.50 sq. ft.   5019. $5.75 sq. ft.   5020. $6.00 sq. ft.

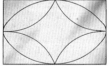

5021. $6.00 square foot   5022. $6.00 square foot

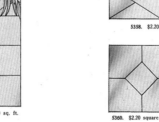

5023. $7.00 square foot   5024. $6.00 square foot

LEADED CLEAR GLASS
Rules for ordering and further description see general information page

5358. $2.20 square foot   5359. $3.00 square foot

5360. $2.20 square foot   5361. $2.30 square foot   5362. $2.20 square foot

5363. $3.00 square foot   5364. $2.20 square foot   5365. $3.75 square foot

CHAPTER 2

Traditional Beginnings

As do other architects, Frank Lloyd Wright went through a period of learning and development. His earliest designs sprang from traditional architecture and patterns learned from a variety of sources, including books, historical buildings, and colleagues in the architectural community.

For example, in his *Autobiography*, Wright relates that the drawings he showed to Sullivan at his employment interview were interpreted from Owen Jones's 1856 *Grammar of Ornament*. Furthermore, it was no surprise when Carter Manny, then head of Chicago's Graham Foundation, came forward with a copy of an 1886 German publication, *Kunstverglasungen*, that was once owned by Wright. There were pencil marks on some pages, and it was clear that the combination of two designs, plates 72 and 74, comprised the design for the second-floor windows and door panels of the entry of his first independent design, the 1893 Winslow House.

Wright used the same pattern with a blue glass border in the 1895 dining room bay addition to his own Oak Park house. This series of simple curves, similar to fish scales, is a common geometric form present in every culture, as evidenced in the Jones book.

Window, dining-room bay addition, 1895, Wright House, Oak Park, Illinois. This pattern is identical to that of the second-floor windows of the earlier Winslow House (facing, inset). This is unusual in Wright's work because he very rarely duplicated a design from one house to another.

Facing: Second-floor plaster frieze, Winslow House, 1893, River Forest, Illinois. The pattern is set on a square diamond sequence but oriented vertically. Although the form of the leaves is very much in the Sullivanesque style, the central sets of balls are additions by Wright that Sullivan would not have used. The leaves are very lifelike and are not conventionalized as they would be in Wright's later work.

Inset: Second-floor window, Winslow House. The pattern is repeated on the interior doors of the Winslow House entry. This has the continuous texture of the frieze and the same kind of vision panel as the Winslow dining room bay, but in this case the clear panel is the entire lower sash.

Part of the character and culture of the client is often reflected in the details and design of the building; a high degree and refinement of details also indicates a client's wealth, and so it was in 1890s Chicago.

Other early patterns that Wright produced also seem to have little of his later innovations. The pattern found in the front entry door and window of the McArthur House are simple fields of tangential circles. Wright's addition beyond what had been used in the preceding several hundred years was the simple border around each light. In the front corner bays, Wright used another simple geometric form, the diamond pane.

Living room bay, interior, Warren McArthur House, 1893, Chicago, Illinois. Any ambiguity of the location of the plane of the lightscreen is removed with the introduction of the diamond pattern. The scale of the pattern does not cause the view to the outside to be obscured. The bay, which adds to the perceived space of the room, is outside the walls, which are on a continuous plane below the bay.

Living room bay, exterior, Warren McArthur House. The original reflection from the diamond panes helps to obscure the view to the interior, but the newer storm windows make it difficult to see this original intent. The cantilever of the window bay adds to the importance of the lightscreens.

Facing: Front door, George Blossom House, 1893, Chicago, Illinois. The field of circles appears to be "cut" from a larger field of circles and into the shape of the half-round opening. There is no relationship between the shape of the opening and the pattern of the glass. The border simply follows the edges of the opening.

Entry, George Blossom House. This design could be found in the colonial pattern books often resourced by more-traditional architects. The circle pattern is unlike that used by Sullivan. The fanlight above the front door appears to be copied directly from a pattern book, as it is a familiar design.

Below, left: Dining room bay, George Blossom House. It is proportioned to a six-by-nine repetition within the frame, but appears to extend past or into the frame due to the manner in which the cames continue to the edges. The little "x"s at the corners are the easiest ones to see. Compare this to the Pindars House (p. 3).

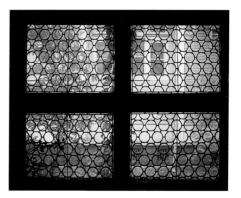

Window at entry, Warren McArthur House, 1893, Chicago, Illinois. Because the lightscreens are hand assembled, the planes of the individual glass surfaces are not perfectly coplanar. The light reflected from the slightly different angles obscures the view into the interior. The pattern of circles is set into a hexagonal arrangement with half circles at all the edges. The single strip of border glass is subdivided by the regularity of the geometry.

Cut-wood screen, dining room, Frank Lloyd Wright House, 1895, Oak Park, Illinois. This is the earliest extant example of Wright's indirect lighting through a large (about 4' x 8') wood lightscreen. A fiberglass rice paper-like diffuser behind the wood fretwork helps to even out the light.

Wright's Early Cut-Wood Screens

Wright's first project at Adler & Sullivan's was for the Auditorium Building. In this building, Sullivan designed several sets of cut-wood screens, including those for the ceiling lights in the main dining hall located on the top floor of the Michigan Avenue side. Wright adapted designs from the dining room of the Auditorium for his own Oak Park house in the barrel vault and cut-wood screens in the 1895 Playroom addition as well as in the new dining room ceiling. In *Grammar of Ornament* under the Byzantine section, plate no. 1, drawing no. 8 is a close approximation to Wright's dining room screen.

Wright used wood screens or grilles in several of his early buildings, apparently borrowing ideas from fellow architects. For instance, the screen door of William Winslow's neighbor Chauncey Williams has a wood grille hinged onto it. At Wright's Moore House, across the street from his own, he designed a wood grille in place of obscure glass for the door between the kitchen and the entry hall. As an adjunct to the cut fretwork of these screens, the closely spaced turned spindles of his balusters often acted as screens.

In Wright's *Autobiography*, he relates that "Cecil [Corwin] and I had a draughting room, each, either side of the common central room for business. Defending this room was an ante-room or vestibule with the ceiling dropped down to the top of the doors. A straight-line glass pattern formed this ceiling glass, diffusing artificial light. The effect of this indirect lighting in the small anteroom was like sunlight, no fixtures visible" (page 123, 1943 edition). Indeed, this may have been the first instance of indirect lighting. Disappointingly, no drawings or photographs exist to show us what must have been an innovative design.

The patterns used in the playroom and dining room ceilings of Wright's home are very much along the Sullivan line. They are a bit more simple than Sullivan, but that is where Wright is expert at simplification.

Balusters, Frank Lloyd Wright House, 1895, Oak Park, Illinois. These close-set balusters comprise a pattern that does more than hold the railing in place.

Wood door grille, Nathan Moore House, 1895, Oak Park, Illinois. The bilaterally symmetrical design is more common in Sullivan's cut-wood patterns than in Wright's lightscreens. The motifs used here are commonly used in his other wood screens for his own house and for the Chauncey Williams House.

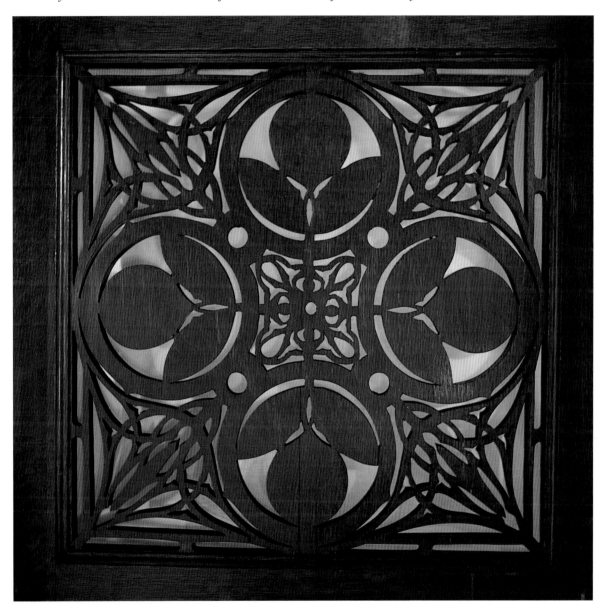

Overleaf: Dining room, Frank Lloyd Wright House, 1895, Oak Park, Illinois. The ceiling lightscreen is backlit by several incandescent lightbulbs, with no daylight from above. It is the second example of this technique, the first being used at the Garrick Theater building he shared with Cecil Corwin. The combination of circles and abstract oak leaves are extensions of the patterns developed by Sullivan for the Auditorium Building and were used again later in the Carson Pirie Scott department store. **41**

Beginnings of Wright's Borders

One idea that came out of these traditional beginnings that developed later was the heavily bordered window. In the windows of Wright's own playroom addition, the basic pattern is a most traditional square pane. Here, Wright introduces an area at the center of each window containing a clear rectangle that would be enlarged in his later work. The dining room windows of the Winslow House exhibit an intricate pattern around a rectangle of this vertical window. When aligned as a set in the semicircular bay, the clear panels take on a horizontal effect. This florid pattern is an adaptation, in glass, of the plaster frieze that surrounds the second floor's exterior.

One of the earliest art-glass patterns of Wright's own design, not based on traditional forms or those that were developed by others around him, was for the George Furbeck House in Oak Park, 1897. The design is a series of three vertical lines at the center with a simple colored border. The window is very narrow and tall. Comparing this to the Heller House of the same year, which employs innovative technology, one wonders why the Furbeck windows are so uninteresting. Not every design is a great work of art, and the architect must also accept significant input from the client. An artist must start somewhere, and Furbeck may well have been the starting point for Wright's glass border art.

While Wright was one who could quickly develop an idea, he had to have a point of beginning as all artists must have. That he began with very traditional forms, patterns, and materials makes his fully developed work even more remarkable. It shows his understanding of line and color as well as a basic knowledge of the proper application of the materials in common use at the time.

Top: Dormer window, Playroom addition, Wright House, 1895, Oak Park, Illinois. These are simpler and more severe than the Winslow dining-room windows while having the same effect as a bordered vision panel. The bay windows just below these were originally the same design but were replaced later with a newer design when the windows were broken by Wright's children and their friends while playing. The remaining unbroken panels were placed in new bookcases flanking the fireplace.

Right: Dining-room window, George Furbeck House, 1897, Oak Park, Illinois. This may be the first of Wright's geometric designs using his T-square and triangle for the pattern rather than the freehand designs with circles and curves. The quiet design may have been at the request of the client and not completely of Wright's making.

Dining room bay, exterior, Winslow House, 1893, River Forest, Illinois. The four horizontal bracing rods fit neatly into the design and are nearly invisible. The storm windows misrepresent the original size of each window.

Below: Dining room bay, interior, Winslow House. This photograph is from the days when the Winslows still lived in the house. The low ceiling and the window seat add to the horizontality of the whole design—not just a single window but the combination of the full set across the entire bay. The lightscreen gives the impression of privacy and security in an area that is open on all three sides.

Dining-room window, interior detail, Winslow House. The dragonfly-wing pattern is very dense and shrouds the view, so the clear central panel is critical to having a view from the interior. At this point in Wright's career, he did not understand the nature of the lead and glass materials as well as he would with more experience. The result was that this pattern was defined by the came alone rather than being in concert with the clear glass. There are two borders for this pattern: the blue opalescent and the clear border at the edge of the wood frame are nearly the same size.

CHAPTER 3

First Experiments in Materials

From the start, Wright seemed to have been interested in the newest developments in technology. His buildings reflect that interest subtly, not in a brutal, industrial way.

Wright's interest in new technologies came about partly through his associations with particular clients. The first to launch him in this direction was probably William H. Winslow, who not only was Wright's first client but who had typeset and printed the first *House Beautiful* on a press in his basement with Wright's assistance in production and design. Winslow also had patented several processes, and in 1897 had invented with his neighbor and Luxfer Prism Company co-incorporator Edward Waller the electro-glazing method that launched the Luxfer company. Wright was the architectural consultant to the company and its link to most of Chicago's architectural community.

Dining room laylight, Ward W. Willits House, 1902, Highland Park, Illinois. This pattern is one of the more simple designs of Wright's work but is very complex, incorporating more than two hundred individual pieces of glass. If one examines the herringbone sections that run perpendicular to each other through the center, one can see there is no came between the glass pieces. The compression by the other cames and glass holds the pieces in place. Part of the success of this assembly is due to the copper colonial cames, which are quite strong. This is one of the first instances where Wright begins to vary the line weights within a design. The herringbone pattern continues into adjacent laylights, and this is one of the first of his patterns to extend into adjacent lights.

Designs without Cames

Although wonderful technological innovations in came were evident in the Heller House and in some of Wright's designs for Luxfer Prism, Wright could also design with the antithesis in mind. For instance, there are two prime examples of his eliminating the metal between pieces in art glass: the MacArthur dining-room remodeling and the Willits House laylights. The elimination of came was Wright's first attempt to vary the line weight of his designs. Later he found other, more waterproof, methods.

In the 1901 dining-room remodeling of the Warren McArthur House in the Kenwood neighborhood of Chicago, Wright included small areas of glass cut into small pieces and assembled with cames only at the ends of the pieces. Since the scale of the pattern was small, the lack of came is hardly noticeable. In the laylights of the entry and dining room of the Willits House of the next year, the use of glass

Doors, Warren McArthur House, 1893, Chicago, Illinois. The small medallions at the top of the doors use parallelogram pieces of glass as part of the pattern. Some of these pieces have came on only two of the four sides. They are held by the ends rather than the sides, as is common. The came used here is lead, and the plane is warped in several areas, resulting in pieces becoming loose and, in a few cases, falling out. Having leaded glass in a door is a maintenance problem for two reasons: the door can flex more than a window, and the impact of a slammed door creates additional stress.

Facing: Stairway window, Isadore Heller House, 1897, Chicago, Illinois. This pattern is a refinement of the Winslow dining room and Wright's original 1895 playroom windows with the clear-glass center panel and border design. Note that the edge border is clear, not opalescent green.

extra metallum (Latin, "without metal") is much more pronounced and noticeable. Through the center of the pattern is a herringbone figure that used the same cameless technique. Both use controlled breaks in individual pieces, resulting in a visible line, but no metal holds them in place. This Willits design signals a major step in the variations in line weight and hints at the graphic effects that are possible in art glass.

Luxfer Prism's Electro-glazing

Electro-glazing, initially patented by Luxfer Prism Company, was a process of inserting a thin ribbon of copper foil instead of lead came between the pieces of glass. The assembled window was plunged into a zinc bath where an electric charge was applied. The zinc in the solution attached itself to the copper and built up molecule by molecule, sealing the space and making a very strong joint. The joint was also very thin, the feature in which Wright was most interested. It appears that this may well have been the

Luxfer prisms, 1897. Luxfer prisms spread quickly throughout the U.S. and Europe. Wright designed many prism plate patterns, but fewer than five different ones were actually manufactured. Number 321 was the least common and number 322 the most common.

process used on the stairway windows of the Heller House, designed in 1897, the same year the Luxfer Prism Company began. The electro-glazing must have been expensive since the company switched to standard zinc cames within a few years.

As the architectural consultant for the Luxfer Prism Company, Wright designed forty-four prism plates. Standard prism patterns may have been taken from Jones's *Grammar of Ornament*, with the Moresque No. 1, drawing 15 being the most popular. The basis for a good number, and possibly all, of Wright's patterns for the Luxfer prism plates could be found in the Jones book if one were to do a comprehensive review. It was apparently a rich source for Wright's early ornamentation, perhaps a greater influence than Sullivan's more modern examples.

Glass Mosaics in Fireplaces

In traditional fireplaces up through the mid-1800s, surrounds were quite often covered with glazed tiles; the Arts & Crafts movement made brick surrounds popular, the same brick used for the exterior of the house. This is the idea that Wright often employed throughout his career. But early on, he experimented with glass-mosaic fireplace surrounds. He used only one glass-mosaic design—the

Plate from Giannini & Hilgart brochure, no date (circa 1906?). This example from the Giannini & Hilgart promotional brochure shows a portion of their showroom with a wide range of pieces produced by the firm. The fireplace in the surround is identical to that of the Husser, Martin, and Ennis Houses, except for their proportions. In all examples, the tree trunk is on the left and there is a clear horizon line. The pottery pieces are manufactured by the Teco company, and some of these pieces were designed by Giannini for Teco. The cabinet doors are typical of other designs presented in the brochure.

Leaf detail, glass-mosaic fireplace surround, Los Angeles house. The leaves in the wisteria mosaics are exactly the shape and style of those in the Martin House. The crackled gold used on the leaves is also consistent between the two.

Glass-mosaic fireplace overmantel, Charles Ennis House, 1925, Los Angeles, California. The Ennis House was not well maintained over the 1940s and '50s. There is a considerable amount of damage repair, done at different times and with varying degrees of success. The exact process used in the original manufacture has not been determined, but The Judson Studios are trying to replicate the method for restoration applications.

wisteria vine—and incorporated it into three different houses, the first being the Joseph J. Husser House, 1899. The mosaic was designed by Blanche Ostertag and executed by Orlando Giannini, who later founded the glass-making firm of Giannini & Hilgart. Robert Spencer's article in the June 1900 issue of the *Architectural Review* shows this fireplace surround, the only representation of it that still exists since the house has been destroyed.

The figure was a conventional wisteria vine with flowers of soft lavenders and pinks. The wisteria was a very popular plant in the Victorian culture, a climbing leguminous shrub with pendant racemes in various colors in blue-violet, white, purple, or rose. In the design, a line separating dull from shiny gold glass tiles appeared to represent the horizon and gave depth to the composition. The trunk was made from several colors of brown and dull gold glass. The leaves had an application of gold leaf that crackled, or broke into tiny fragments over the surface. The flower forms are the most representational.

The D. D. Martin House, 1904, of Buffalo, New York, received the second and by far the largest glass mosaic, also executed by Giannini. The glass mosaic for the Charles Ennis House, 1924, Los Angeles, was the third and last. Other glass-mosaic wisteria examples, though not associated to Wright, include the Edward A. Probst House in River Forest; the Blinn House in Pasadena, by an early Wright associate, George Washington Maher; and another for an anonymous house of about 1914 in Los Angeles. Probst worked for Daniel Burnham and was one of the named partners in the successor firm of Graham, Anderson, Probst and White.

All of these examples are virtually the same—the same pattern and position of elements, same technology, and same glass colors. Could all have come from the same source? Are they Wright's design and Giannini's technology? Or were they all designed by Ostertag, manufactured by Giannini & Hilgart, then purchased to supplement the house designs? The answer is unknown at this point.

In the two catalogs published for Giannini & Hilgart, there are two designs for wisteria fireplace surrounds. One is very similar to Wright's design. The crackled-gold technique was pending a patent by Giannini about 1904, but there is no evidence that one was ever granted to him.

There were many other styles and patterns of glass-mosaic fireplace surrounds produced by Giannini and other Chicago art-glass firms, including Linden (and the Spierling & Linden Decorating Company, a sister company to the Linden Art Glass firm).

Studio, offices and workshops, Linden Glass Company and Spierling & Linden, Chicago, Illinois. This was the location (now demolished) for the Linden Glass Company and its sister Spierling & Linden Company for most of their long life.

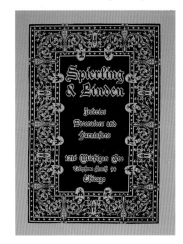

Advertisement, Spierling & Linden, Chicago, Illinois. This was the sister company of the Linden Glass Company in which Mr. Linden participated.

Entry fireplace, Darwin D. Martin House, 1904, Buffalo, New York. It is possible that Darwin Martin saw the Husser House on one of his Chicago trips and requested it for his house, but no evidence has been found. The Martin fireplace mosaic presented a greater challenge than the Husser mosaic because of its size and proportion. Outside corners had to be carefully detailed, and the glass on the short ends would be subject to abrasion and impact due to their being parts of the doorways between rooms. It must have been the most impressive feature of the house, among many impressive features both built-in and freestanding.

Trunk detail, glass-mosaic fireplace surround, Los Angeles house. This house was not designed by Wright, but the same glass is used in this case as was used in the Martin House and all the other fireplaces. It would be almost impossible for every one of these installations to have been created individually and still have glass in the trunk, background gold, and crackled-gold leaves in the exact colors of glass as in these examples. It seems logical to assume that all came from the same source. Was it possible that the Giannini & Hilgart firm sold these glass surrounds to other art-glass firms to complete and install?

Wisteria vine at the D. D. Martin House, 1904, Buffalo, New York. This vine once grew outside the living room of the Martin House. Its colors are those that Wright and Giannini used for the amazing installation of the fireplace surround.

Remnants, glass-mosaic fireplace surround, D. D. Martin House, 1904, Buffalo, New York. These are the few remaining of the thousands of pieces from the two-sided entry and living-room fireplace in the Martin House. While the house was abandoned for about fifteen years from circa 1935 to 1950, water leaked in, causing most of the mosaics to fall to the floor. The next owner, never having seen the original beauty of the surround, tossed most of the small pieces into the trash. These few pieces make clear the techniques of glazing and firing used by Giannini in these wisteria fireplace surrounds and give a hint of its original beauty.

Most of these glass mosaics were composed of cut glass arranged in a pattern. The glass mosaics used in Wright's installations were all fired after they were cut. Some had the crackled-gold Giannini finish but others did not. The refiring softens the edges much like a chocolate bar left in the sun too long.

Interestingly, Wright did not create ceramic fireplace surrounds, even though this material had been in use for several centuries. Such an example exists in the Mess House, designed by former Wright associate Walter Burley Griffin. This design, depicting a rural scene, is not any more representational than the wisteria. Wright may have preferred glass because of the depth of the color as well as the sparkle.

Wright began to explore possibilities in materials in a vigorous manner and when he could convince his client of its benefits. Most of Wright's clients were technically inclined and it may not have been much of a task, but the results gave Wright the reassurance and experience to make advances in the materials with which he enjoyed designing. Others were dropped from his palette. With the network of clients, those that were acquainted with each other outside of Wright's circle may have seen the examples and requested some of these designs for their own houses.

Fireplace, Mess House, 1913, Winnetka, Illinois, Walter Burley Griffin, architect. This ceramic fireplace surround is one of the few in a Prairie house. The quiet colors and serene scene offset the severe lines and coarse texture of the quarter-sawn white-oak trim. Ceramic lacks the sparkle and depth of color that Wright's glass mosaic had.

CHAPTER 4

First Successes in Pattern

Wright left traditional patterns behind and began to follow his own style about 1900. His development of lightscreens paralleled his search for new forms in his architecture. His work now seemed to exude more confidence than it did earlier. As his ideas and approaches took form, Wright's creative energy emerged with tremendous power. He could hardly contain himself and took on more work than anyone could possibly produce at the level of design and detail to which he was inclined. But producing unusual, innovative buildings puts a lot of pressure on a designer. He had to educate his staff, contractors, and craftsmen in order to carry out his wishes.

Wright's work can be studied along two lines of development: one is the bordered design and the other is the full texture, or overall, design. The work in these designs is unique and more personal than those of even two or three years earlier. At age thirty-three in 1900, Wright was able to see design possibilities quicker than most young designers. The new specifications were complex and must have been detailed to a greater degree than the standard specifications in common use at the time. Wright's executed patterns at this point still appear to have been drafted, and he was not as adept as he would later become at the design of glass material and its positive/negative values. Patterns are more abstract than earlier ones, although these are abstractions of plant

Facing: Living room bay window, B. Harley Bradley House, 1900, Kankakee, Illinois. The patterns clearly include both the upper and lower units. The bottom of the upper design is included at the top of the lower unit in an awkward balance, making the total appear to be top-heavy. The red accents at each of the abstract tulips hardly draw attention.

materials—native flowers, and weeds—not just geometrical constructions. The designs were often extensions of the kinds of things Wright photographed himself, such as the prairie aster.

Bradley House

The Bradley House (1900) window is likely the first glass design that was related to a building design. The pitch of the roof 4 in 12 is reflected in the angles of parts of the glass design.

It is likely that the Bradley House lightscreens were designed before those of its neighbor, the Hickox House (1900). The windows are constructed of lead came and white milk-glass flowers —with ruby red accents above. Each panel has a complete border and multiple repetitions of flowers twice in the top pane and once in the bottom—and a vertical band of squares in the center top. One way to tell that Wright was drafting his designs and not considering the materials he was using is to take note of the use of L glass pieces. The geometry of the L makes the inside corner a natural place for a stress point that is quite likely to cause a glass break. Most of the L pieces in the Bradley windows are cracked at just this point. In fact, once Wright understood this problem, he discontinued using the L shape.

The Bradley window continues the pattern from the lower panel to the sash above but does not continue it from one window to the next at its side. All six units of the bay window have the same design. The upper panel has a pattern at center, while the bottom panel has a border. The installation is unusual in that the windows go clear to the ceiling and do not have a normal head height (more than one foot of wall above windows six feet eight inches in a room with ceilings eight feet or more; here, the ceiling is nine feet. To accomplish this, the high window required a complicated and unusual construction detail to allow for the proper structural framing.

The dining room ceiling laylights have a reverse pattern relationship. The crossbars align with each orientation. This is a rudimentary method to establish a relationship between two panels. The triangular head detail and the horizontal accents to each side of it give an American Indian effect to the pattern, almost an abstracted eagle. The red lines are too small and do not have enough contrast with the other dark glass used throughout the panels to have much impact. There is no relationship to the windows except for a central symmetrical pattern. This ceiling laylight has a section at either side of the triangular head that has no came between the horizontal pieces. The heavy linear pattern is confusing and appears to be just a jumble of lines. The use of lead instead of stronger colonial came shapes does not produce the precision that this linear design requires. The V head is too close to the edge and needs the border for relief, as Wright had done frequently before this. The top medallions at either side of the V head are set into the field of glass without regard for construction and introduce another L glass section. Surprisingly, and perhaps because the glass is set into a horizontal frame instead of a vertical window, none of these L pieces are broken.

Dining-room-ceiling laylight, B. Harley Bradley House, 1900, Kankakee, Illinois. This photograph was taken while the laylights were in their original position, showing the location and effect of the incandescent lights behind the screen. At first glance, one might not notice that each pane contains reversed images.

Hickox House

Parallel diagonal lines are offset from one another and establish a pure abstraction of borders in the Hickox windows. There is no color in this design, only white milk glass at a few joints. As with the Bradley House windows, the diagonals are angled the same as the pitch of the roof. This pattern is more sophisticated than those of the Bradley House and with the diagonals, more dynamic. Wright uses a hexagonal medallion window within an octagonal bay of the building. He mixes geometries in proximity and makes it work without a sense of conflict that one might expect. Each unit within the sash and the extension of the came into the frame begin to indicate that the pattern will extend through and into the next sash, coordinating the two. This is a very important part of the design and gives the lightscreen highlight and impact. The piece is carefully framed in the wood surround, enhanced by the double sill at the bottom.

Living room window, Warren Hickox House, 1900, Kankakee, Illinois. The thin, vertical milk glass at the center of each unit appears to be a muntin bar, part of the architecture, integrating the glass and the building.

Transoms and door,
Hickox House, 1900,
Kankakee, Illinois. Four units
above with a pair of doors
below show how adaptable the
hexagonal design can be and
how well Wright is able to con-
trol the proportions of the
common elements.

Thomas House

The Thomas House (1901) pattern is clearly an abstraction of plant materials—a complex series of small squares and adjoining rectangles. The use of lead and contrasting, sharp, gold mirror glass adds to the excitement of the design. The heads, composed of three narrow isosceles triangles, are balanced with wider and complex tails. The extended tails of the doors include nearly opaque lines—two on the entry doors and three on the porch door. Unlike other windows, the Thomas House windows each have an opalescent border. Most of the glass is clear. The alternate, which Wright used in many other windows, would have been to create an opalescent border near the edge and have a clear edge. Someone has installed horizontal bracing bars at the tails to bolster weak lead (unlike the copper-camed tails in the Willits House, which needed no such support).

Living room window series, Frank Thomas House, 1901, Oak Park, Illinois. As with many of Wright's ribbon windows (many windows set next to each other in a row), what began as a pattern of vertical units with vertical patterns has been overtaken by a horizontal effect once the assembly has been completed.

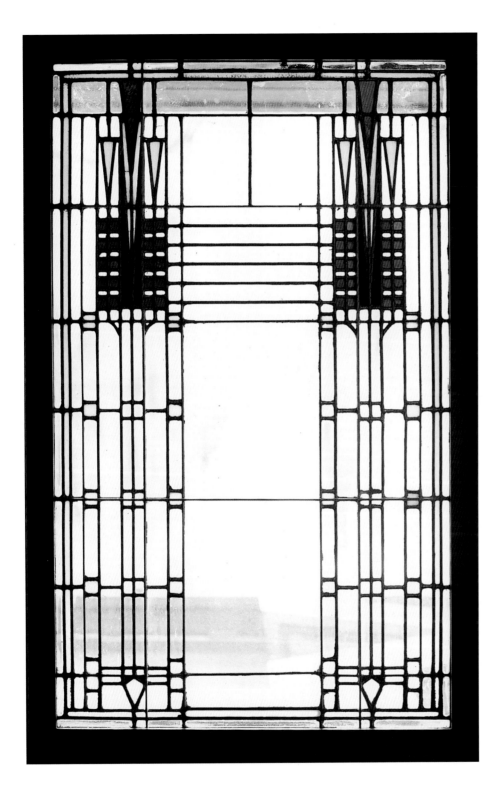

Left: Living room window, Frank Thomas House. This pattern is the basis for all the exterior doors and windows throughout the house. A new crossbar introduced at a point one-third of the way from the bottom to strengthen the lead came has altered the original design. The pattern is a more complex elaboration of the one at the Willits House.

Below: Second-floor window, Frank Thomas House. The three-part window design had been used on Chicago's commercial buildings for twenty years prior to construction of the Thomas House. But with a large, clear central window flanked by smaller ones on each side, the pattern here becomes symmetrical within the sidelights.

Above: Entry-vestibule doors, Frank Thomas House. The vestibule becomes a crystal room with lightscreens on three sides and lit from above; incandescent lights and mother-of-pearl appliqués create the pattern.

Right: Living room door and window, Frank Thomas House. The sidelights are developed along with those of the second-floor windows. The three-panel pattern of the door includes opaque gold glass, giving a balance to the flourishes at the top of the door.

64

W. E. Martin House

This lightscreen in the W. E. Martin House (1902) is a simple pattern like a grille. The same base pattern is used in the fountain doors at the Dana House (1904) (see p. 78), but a cascading plant flows over the grille, which acts as a trellis. This is Wright's first successful use of thick and thin came together. The thicker came does not overpower the thin came, and the combination of the two gives each a scale.

Wright includes a sophisticated joint flourish with squares, rectangles, and opalescent glass. The three borders at the sides and only two at the top and bottom create a bilateral asymmetry. Horizontal vision panels are used in the center of the design, but came also runs through the center. Division of the border at the center top and bottom—an uncommon visual device—prevents the lines from visually spreading or joining together. Corners are highlighted with opalescent glass. The proportion of each glass piece is good, with not too many or too few elements. The alignment of thick and thin came at the edge of the large came adds to the continuity. This is a dynamic design, even with straight lines and ninety-degree angles. The tension is expressed almost as if the thick cames that span across the center of the window are stretched across it and are attached at the edges of the frame.

Bedroom window, William E. Martin House, 1902, Oak Park, Illinois. This represents one of Wright's earliest uses of double-crown came. The delicate vertical lines, inboard of the frame, give contrast and balance as well as a stopping point for the horizontal milk glass along the outside.

Davenport House

A carryover from the Thomas House is the overall grille, or screen, of the Davenport House (1901). Davenport is one of the few commissions Wright took with a partner, in this case Webster Tomlinson. There are design complications at both the top and bottom: a higher density of lead detail. The use of lead makes the piece weaker, and the lines are not as straight after a hundred years as they once were. The glass is original to the house but was in a bay window before remodeling.

The wood screen at the entry gives a preview of the glass screens in the rest of the house, all Japanese in feeling.

Wood entry screen, Arthur Davenport House, 1901, River Forest, Illinois. The closely spaced wood spindles create a visual screen at the entry for the house. The surrounding wood details complete the Japanese effect of the composition.

Left: Living room window, Arthur Davenport House. The much shorter pattern retains the same graphic effect as the taller living room units.

Living room windows, Arthur Davenport House. The closely placed lead cames create a heavy screen that is only slightly relieved at the center by half as many cames as at the top and bottom. This pattern is symmetrical and would produce the same effect if inverted.

CHAPTER 5

Success in Materials

After about ten years in practice on his own, Wright had developed a unique, personal, and very powerful system of lightscreen design. In the Dana House—knowing that he had the freedom to design without regard to budget—Wright finally came into his own. He seemed to be the only artist working in glass and metal who understood the graphic effects possible using the full palette of these materials. While most designers thought of the metal only as a way to hold the glass pieces in position, Wright treated it as an important part of the design.

Round-headed front door of the Susan Lawrence Dana House, 1904, Springfield, Illinois. Above this window is the fanlight with the butterfly motif.

Left: Entry door and fanlight, Francis Little House, 1904, Peoria, Illinois. The round-headed door is reminiscent of the Dana House door, which was designed and drafted at exactly the same time. Instead of using iridescent straw glass as in the Dana House, the palette was clear plate glass and opaque gold mirror glass, which is comprised of two pieces of glass placed back to back, with gold applied between for a mirror finish. Very little is known about the technique for getting the gold mirror on both sides of the glass. When the seal is broken this gold deteriorates.

While the Dana door was a single sheet of clear plate glass, the Little House door has an art-glass screen pattern. The Little door pattern and the fanlight pattern are unrelated except for the materials used, which are different from those used for the remainder of the exterior windows. The came in the door and fanlight are the thin rolled sheets, like those manufactured by Chicago Metallic Company. Here they are brass and have acquired a black patina.

Facing: Detail of reception-room window, Darwin D. Martin House, 1904, Buffalo, New York. The specifications given to Linden Glass Company by Wright have never been located. Wright may have conveyed his instructions in person during a visit to their Michigan Avenue studio. He is said to have reviewed each sheet and color of glass in detail with the studio head. The result is spectacular. Wright understood nature in many unspoken ways. He knew that a single color of green glass in the checkerboard would not imbue the lightscreen with the life that these variegated greens give it.

Overlapping butterflies are unique in Wright's work. Using only straight lines, he was able to construct an image that one imagines to be in graceful curving arcs and circles. Here Wright absorbs the essence of the object and gives back the essential qualities in a geometricized form.

The abdomen is rather generic but is given some volume and substance by the addition of diagonal lines. The taper of the abdomen is the only departure from strict right-angle geometry.

Wright gives a dynamic view by varying the density of color in opposing wings. This attention to the whole comes across in his inclusion of antennae along the outer edge of the pattern.

The mastery of this design results more from the materials than the pattern. The glass that he chose has a delicate iridescence close to the beautiful qualities of luminescence often found in exotic butterflies. The white parallelograms at the shoulders both reflect and refract light in contrast to the other glass used in the remainder of the wing.

Besides the use of a living, breathing, animated animal, another departure of the fanlight design is the radial layout. The axis of each butterfly is on the line to the center of the arch. The iridescent arrowhead that separates each butterfly takes up what would be the gap between the angles.

The appearance of the glass Wright chose for these butterflies and for the other art-glass windows in the Dana House changes as the day passes. The harsh midday light makes them appear delicate while the soft light of dawn and dusk defines them sharply in the adjacent clear glass.

Wright's design gives very different impressions, depending on whether it is viewed with reflective light, as in the image below left, or by transmitted light, as shown on the right. His choice of materials was careful, providing ever-changing dimensions to his designs.

The materials used in the butterflies are consistent with those used throughout the Susan Lawrence Dana House. They consist of clear glass, iridescent, variegated straw-amber glass, and copper-coated zinc metal cames.

Between two sets of the butterfly fanlights is a full 180-degree barrel vault of art glass. The serenity of the butterfly design is contrasted with the dynamism of the barrel vault. As one passes through these arches and vaults, there is a profusion of art glass, almost too much to take in on the short walk. The lightbulbs behind the barrel vault help to minimize the contrast in light level between the outside and the inside. Wright was introducing a type of light that one would experience if one passed below a branch during a walk in the woods, a favorite idea and pastime of Wright's. All through the Dana House are sets of overhead lights that suggest this dappled forest light.

Entry hanging light, Susan Lawrence Dana House, 1904, Springfield, Illinois. This is one of Wright's earliest hanging light shades. The inverted pyramid extends into space at its point but is more three-dimensional than that with the addition of the subtle fins attached to the hips. The design continues the sumac theme with a quadrennial flower head on each face.

Dining room sumac bay window detail, Susan Lawrence Dana House. Nature is never strictly symmetrical. There are variations within the set. Wright understood this and was able to work with it. In this detail of the sumac design from the Dana dining room bay window, he introduces a regular pattern but interrupts it along its line and at the ends, producing a three-dimensional effect.

It was known that Wright visited the heads of art-glass studios and workers who executed his designs; we can assume that he must have discussed his design ideas with them. This interaction with the artisans probably added to his ability to expand the use of materials that had been around for some years in ways that were understood by none before and few since. The materials with which he was having the most success were zinc, brass, and galvanized-steel came, and cathedral, opalescent, milk, and clear glass.

Especially in the Dana House we see remarkable works of art whose designs feature the versatility of the materials. In one instance in the Dana House studio, he hung the lightscreen just inside a plate-glass window (see facing p. 1), and in the upper dining room he used a similar design as a window.

Dining room sumac bay window, Susan Lawrence Dana House. Wright must have been very convincing when he presented his scheme for the ornamental art-glass windows throughout this elaborate house to his client, Susan Lawrence Dana. Sumac would rarely be considered a thing of beauty to anyone from the Midwest. It would be considered a weed if not a nuisance, but his interpretation of this weed is startlingly beautiful. Leaves and branches of wild sumac usually droop toward the ground. Here Wright takes it in its freest form and makes it upright. He accentuates the pollen and seed head. The coloration reflects only a single aspect and perhaps its most fleeting one—the brilliant fall palette.

73

Dining room chandelier, Susan Lawrence Dana House. There are five of these hanging lights, four identical ones in the dining room and one with minor differences in the turnaround into the Studio room. This is perhaps the most complex of all of Wright's art-glass creations, and it was never repeated. There are four fins, one at each corner framing a simple traditional lantern shape defined at the edges by delicate transparent milk glass. The pattern as defined by the came and the colored glass makes it appear considerably more complex. On the upper face of the lantern, the four iridescent squares that meet the fins appear to change planes and bevel upward, but they do not; they are just set at a different angle within the same plane. The four bottom finials, as well as those at the top and the rods that support the light, are all composed of double-crown came.

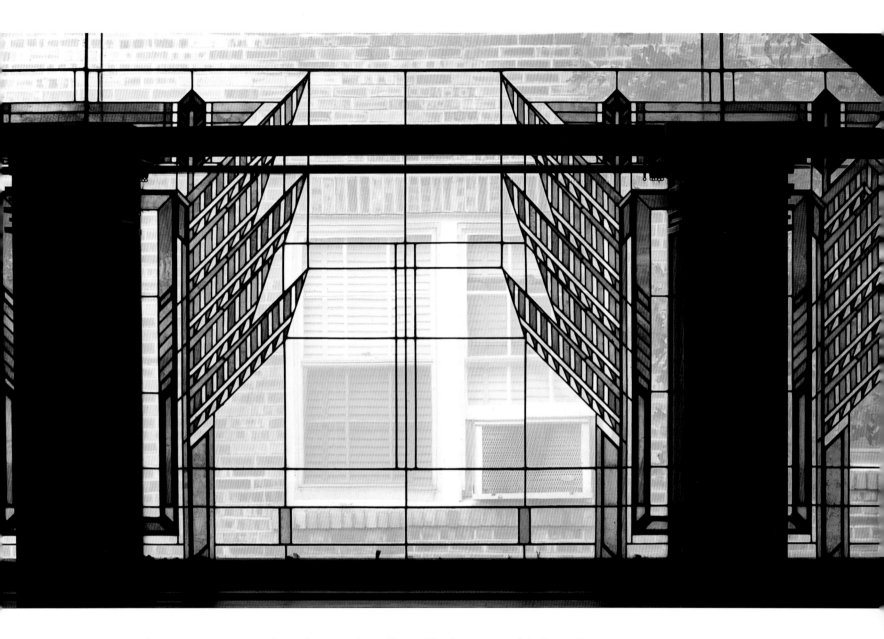

Dining room window interior, upper story, Susan Lawrence Dana House. The dining room of the Dana House is two stories. Unlike the living room, which can be viewed in its entirety from the street, the dining room must be taken in more than one part at a time. The second-story lightscreen is composed of this sumac design, which embraces the architectural elements that pierce the half-round opening, emphasizing the power of the architecture over all else. The sumac pattern is split by the finial extension of the column, although the finial does not extend through the window but stops short and supports a horizontal curtain rod. The first-floor design is a series of identical window units set into a round bay extending well past the plane of the second-floor window.

He also began designing lightscreens as complex three-dimensional fixtures: for use with incandescent sources, he created wall sconces, ceiling fixtures, hanging lights, and table lamps. In at least one instance—the Dana Music Cabinet—the screen was used in a piece of freestanding furniture, though the use of glass patterns in cabinet doors was not a new innovation. Wright's patterns were not limited to self-contained single windows, but he was able to make strong patterns that crossed into as many as seven continuous sections.

Wright was able to anticipate the differences created in his designs by both reflected light from the outside and transmitted light from the inside. For instance, light transmitted through uranium glass would have a visual effect different from light transmitted through silver glass. In addition, Wright could anticipate the differences resulting from the changing qualities of light throughout the year.

Above, right, and top facing: These designs for the Dana House Fountain doors are the finest patterns and use the finest materials Wright ever devised. At first look, the doors appear to be a symmetrical pair. Upon further observation, one realizes the true nature of them: that they are quite different patterns but within limits, such as those in nature. The glass that forms the border along the two is nearly clear and has a faint white milk cast that is at first unnoticeable.

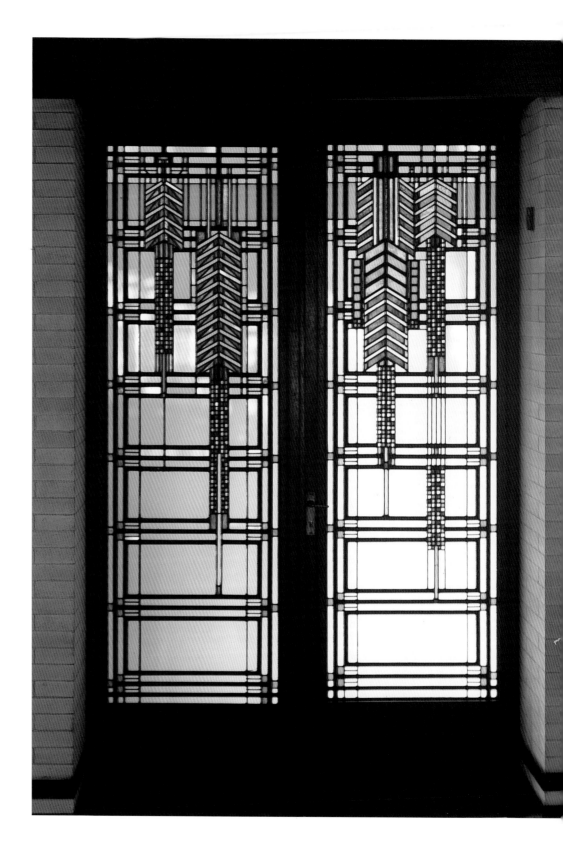

Fernery doors, Dana House. This pattern is nearly identical to and mimics the "framework" that supports the climbing vines of the fountain doors. It is made of double-crown came, as was used in the William E. Martin House.

Double-pedestal lamp. Wright brought the same innovation and enthusiasm to the lighting he designed for many of his houses as he did the architectural and lightscreen design. This photo shows the lamp in its original applied patina, which has since been removed.

Inset: Bedroom window exterior. This is the second-floor top of the design that extends over the entire east facade of the Dana House. It is Wright's only pattern to extend over the entire facade—both first- and second-floor windows—that does not simply repeat the pattern in every window. The most prominent features from the exterior are the large white hexagon at the center and the white parallelograms with line extensions at the top. The colored glass is iridized with wisps of green and blue, blending nicely with the reflections in the clear plate glass from the trees and the sky.

Master-bedroom window, interior, Susan Lawrence Dana House. From the interior, the emphasis shifts to the major and minor seeds, the area of the highest density of detail and came with the straw-colored glass. The pattern achieves a dimensional effect with the side figures apparently in front of the cames that follow the roofline. The double-crown cames (the thickest ones) give both visual and physical strength to the composition, although none of the cames are continuous in a vertical line.

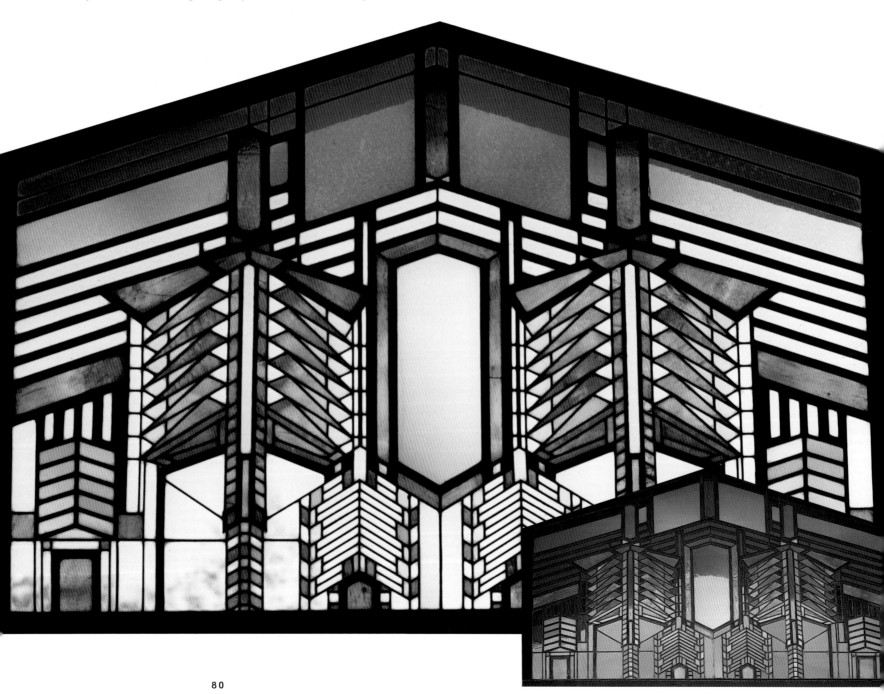

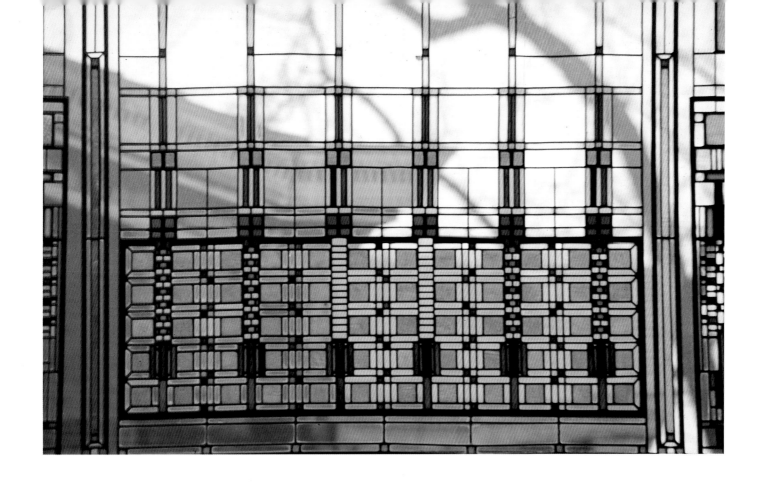

Above: Interior detail, studio hanging lightscreen, Susan Lawrence Dana House. Before restoration, the hanging lightscreen was in a poor state of repair, with several pieces of glass and came missing. Wright had a lot of faith in the strength of the solder joints in this composition. Each of these panels, but especially the center one, is very heavy and is held in place only by hooks attached to the wood supporting frame. The pattern is based on an abstracted corn theme. Individual corn kernels make up the bottom of the panel and corn silk extends into the clear plate above.

Left: Fountain window interior, Susan Lawrence Dana House. On each side of the hallway behind the entry fountain is a series of doors and windows having related designs. This set is known as the fountain doors and the fountain windows. They are unparalleled as the best of Wright's work in glass. The group includes double sets of doors as well as tall narrow windows, some overlooking the backyard and others framing the view into other rooms. Each unit is based on a double-crown frame of trellis with several variations of abstract plant materials intertwined. This smaller composition can stand on its own, as can all the others in the house, and is complete without reference to adjacent units.

Glass in Wright's lightscreens was not intended to alter the color of the light in a room, as, for instance, with the Richardson sun windows mentioned earlier; in fact, colored glass was a minor part of the total lightscreen area. Wright also avoided the most common colors of red, blue, and yellow, preferring earth tones such as amber.

The overall effect of Wright's lightscreens was to make openings in buildings more architectural, not simply rectangles cut in the walls, such as the half-round windows of the Dana House. Some of his windows cannot even be detected from the exterior—for example, the slit windows of the Unity Temple and the Martin House, the half-round windows of the Dana House, and the interruptions that pierce the Dana upper-dining room windows.

The point is not that Wright thought of every possibility that could be accomplished with art glass but that he developed an unprecedented expertise within his range, within his limits of mostly straight lines. No one has surpassed his ability when it comes to designing with straight lines, squares, and rectangles.

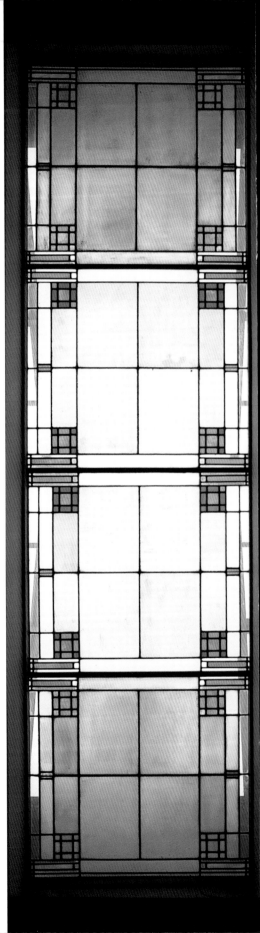

Facing, far left: Stairway window, Unity Temple, 1906, Oak Park, Illinois. Almost invisible from the exterior, a series of windows like this one appear only as shadowed vertical slit defining the corner piers that contain the stairways. These lightscreens extend past the floors, which are held back from the glass and are continuous from top to bottom.

Left: Social-room skylights, Unity Temple. In contrast to the yellow and brown glass used in the temple room, the glass here is much more neutral, being sandblasted obscure glass with green accents. The pattern is a series of repeated squares positioned in several supporting rectangles.

Above: Temple auditorium skylights. This pre-restoration photograph shows the original glass and some obviously later additions. Brown is a difficult color to achieve and to match in glass, but Wright used it to add a little warmth. The design itself is one of Wright's finest compositions of a simple square. The complexity occurs at the point where it contacts the oak trim that tethers it to the ceiling at one side. It certainly would hold the interest of a daydreaming parishioner.

Stairway window, Heath House, 1905, Buffalo, New York. The multi-part design is the first one Wright conceived of extending over several units. The herringbone medallion is not centered within the unit but is offset to one side, allowing for the introduction of the connector line composed of two parallel double-crown cames and white milk glass between them. The connector line extends through the adjacent unit and into a third, in this particular case, the opposite hand of the unit shown. As with the design on the east side of the Dana House, the iridescent glass has a straw color for the base glass and shifts color emphasis to green when viewed from the interior. (An interior view of a portion of the window appears on the back jacket of this book.)

Facing: Interior and exterior of living room window, Frank Barton House, 1903, Buffalo, New York. This is one of the sidelights from the front living room window group, comprised of one clear plate and two matching sidelights. The pattern is a simplified version of several combined from the Dana House. The borders are not strong but carry the proper proportional impact. The glass is similar to that used in the Dana House iridized straw. The came is brass colonial throughout. Most of the windows in this house were original at this writing and have weathered their nearly one hundred years quite well. When viewed from the exterior, the deep-set design blocks the detail at the bottom and shifts the emphasis to the upper medallion. The green of the base glass seen through the iridescent coating applied to it contrasts well with the orange, iron-spot brick.

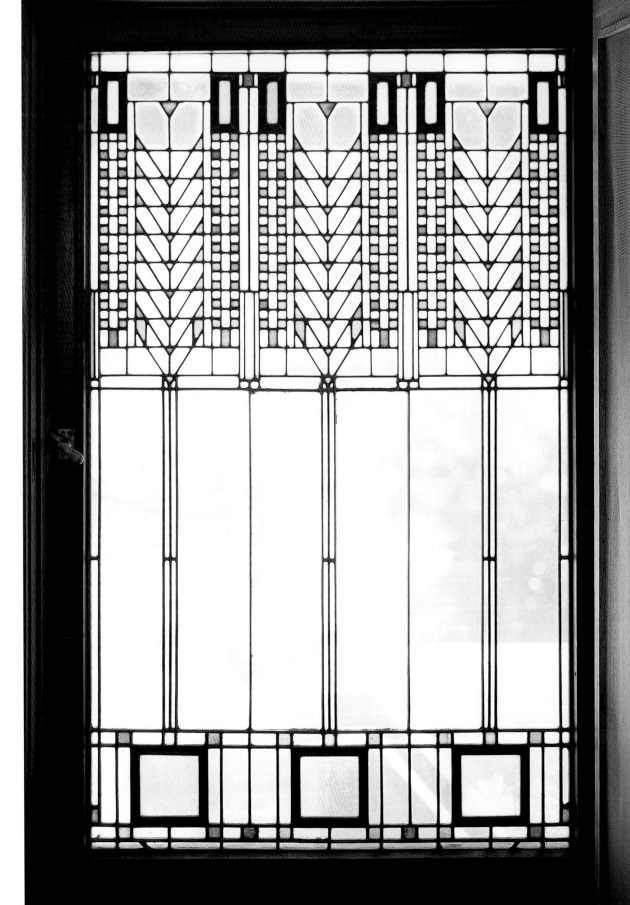

Darwin D. Martin House.
Facing: Master-bedroom window. Above: Radiator windows.

Previous pages and right: Darwin D. Martin House, 1904, Buffalo, New York

Page 86, Master-bedroom window. The popular appeal of this lightscreen design is likely due to its widespread distribution. After Mr. Martin's death, the house was abandoned for fifteen years and many of the precious windows were removed during this time. Unlike other Wright buildings that remained intact, the Martin designs found their way into many prestigious museums and galleries, allowing many more people to see this fine work up close and in person.

The Martins were interested in plants and gardening, having a large conservatory as part of the building. The pattern is of three plants with a square at the roots and many branches above a thin stem. Several art historians have labeled this as a "tree of life" pattern, although there are many elements that do not comply with a standard design of this description. There are too many branches; normally a tree of life has twelve.

As with many other designs, the vertical pattern becomes one of horizontal bands when grouped with other window units. This particular example is from the second-floor master bedroom in its original installation. There are drawings and some correspondence concerning the alteration of this design for the first-floor reception hall, where Darwin Martin eliminates the large squares at the bottom and extends the stem to the bottom border. Mr. Martin said that the large squares obscured his view. Wright had no objections to this alteration.

The cames are the same single- and double-crown cames as used at the Dana and the Barton Houses. The glass is also from the same manufacturer, Kokomo Opalescent Glass Company. It was iridized as well.

Page 87: Radiator windows. At the border between the living room and the dining room to the north and the library to the south, were multiple sets of four brick piers defining the area that contained large radiators. Above oak bookshelves spanning between the brick piers were these windows. This photo is from the east exterior window on the living room side of the library. The total pattern consists of two casement units flanked by tall, thin windows on either side.

These windows use the same straw glass as many of the other windows but gold mirror glass is introduced in these patterns. The emphasis is on the horizontal, as in the William Martin House of just a few years earlier. The band at the bottom spans across the centerline, visually locking the two together. The vertical herringbone at either side of the centerline extends through the bottom band, breaking it with double-crown colonial came.

Right: Bursar's-room window. This pattern is related to the radiator windows from the east side of the house. The bursar's room is on the far west end. There is an indication that they were designed and installed some years later than the completion of the house. Unlike the radiator windows, these have a vertical line, but they have similar density of detail along with the frequent use of gold mirror glass and very little iridescent glass. The design is not particularly indicative of any specific plant and appears to be an abstract pattern.

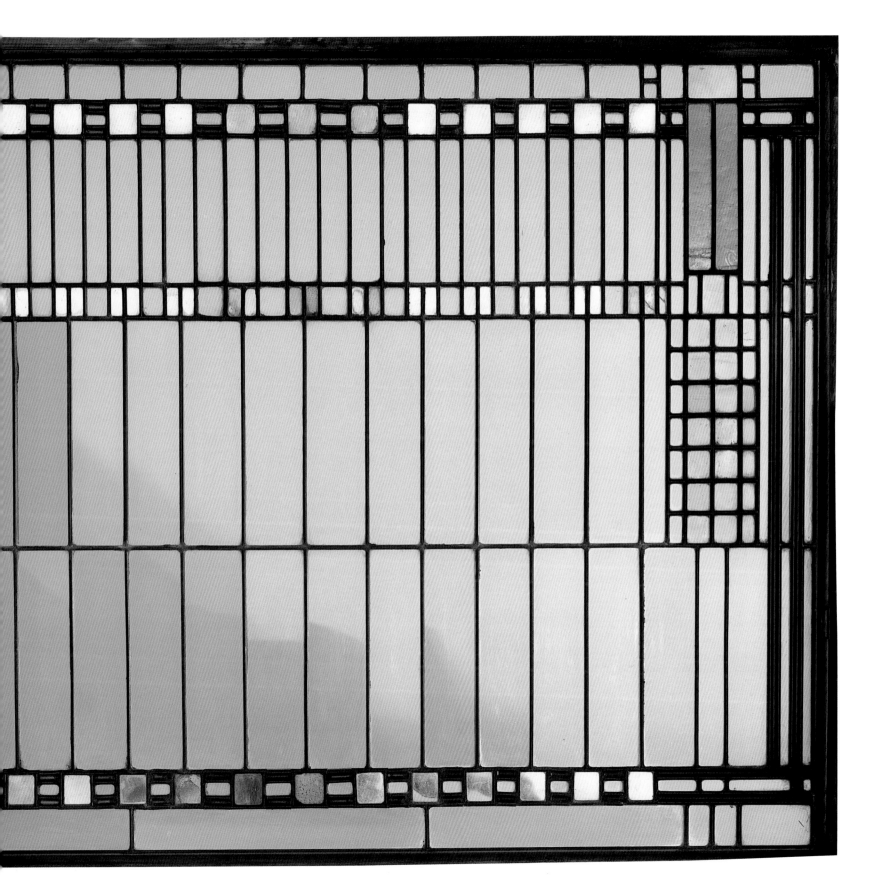

CHAPTER 6

Simple and Less Costly Patterns

Not all of Wright's architectural clients wanted or could afford elaborate lightscreens, he responded with some simple screens. The materials used in these varied from the standard metal came to simple wood muntin bars. Wright also reverted to tried-and-true traditional patterns such as the diamond pane.

One wonders why, at the height of his creativity, Wright would use so common a pattern as the diamond pane found in the Davidson and Millard Houses. There is an indication that, since many glass firms were familiar with diamond panes, they would cost less than other overall patterns. Wright does turn the main axis of the normal pattern ninety degrees putting the diamond on the horizontal rather than the vertical. These windows also have a typical Wright border.

Facing: Window, Emil Bach House, 1915, Chicago, Illinois. The pattern appears to be merely a double-camed frame extending into this window. Flourishes at the upper corner and the bottom edge are mostly straw-colored cathedral glass.

Left: Walter Davidson House, 1908, Buffalo, New York, exterior. Dark glass areas and lighter cames make this pattern more prominent on the exterior than on the interior. The density of the diamond pattern is delicate, a balanced pairing with the smooth stucco.

Right: Davidson interior. From the interior, the window appears larger than it does from the exterior because tall, narrow windows admit a lot of light. They also act as the structural members that hold up the roof.

Hoyt House exterior, 1906. This is one of the least expensive houses of Wright's Prairie years. Hoyt, a pharmacist, requested his initial be included in his distinctively designed house.

Far right: Windows, George M. Millard House, 1906. The diamonds are accented by milk-glass triangles near the edges. The diamonds are at a very large scale, quite unlike those of the Davidson and Roberts Houses.

Living room windows, William B. Greene House, 1912. The simple wood muntins define three squares in the upper half of each window.

Far right: Peter A. Beachy House, 1906. The family story has it that Mrs. Beachy did not want the fussy art glass that her Forest Avenue neighbors were getting from Mr. Wright.

Right: Exterior window detail, Stephen M. B. Hunt House, 1907. At the outside, thin fixed-glass panels allow the full window jamb to be set off from the wall.

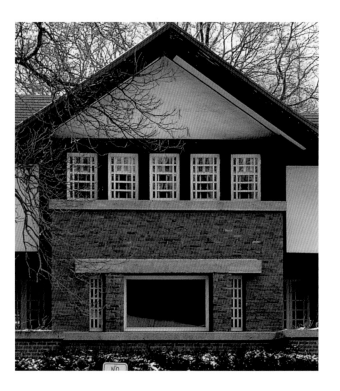

Frederick F. Tomek House,
1907, Riverside, Illinois.

*Upper left: In each individual window unit,
the pattern is divided into three parts, as in the
Darwin D. Martin House (see p. 86). It has
the same top-heavy figure and the small square
at the bottom band. With the increased fre-
quency of decoration at the top, it is obvious
that that the bottom section was intended for
the focused view.*

*Above: Series of living room windows.
As a composition of several pieces, the design
is comprised of horizontal bands in the upper
third, with a much thinner line just above
the bottom. The continuous band of windows
provides the wide view of the prairie that was
so closely associated with Wright's work.*

*Left: Living room-window detail. The initial
T was the centerpiece of each of the three sections of each window.*

Today, several art-glass companies charge by the piece, no matter what the size. Perhaps this is what Wright found. Even in some expensive houses, such as the Robie, the glass pieces are several times larger than those used at both the Dana House and D. D. Martin House. There are well over 600 pieces in the D. D. Martin "tree of life" window, with about ninety in the Tomek (1907) design and only eight in the Greene 1912 example, although all of these windows are about the same size.

The simple designs are not boring or crude. Using fewer pieces of glass gave Wright an opportunity to refine and simplify his abstractions. In fact, creating a simple design with few lines is more difficult because of the delicate balance of proportion and scale.

On the windows with wood muntin bars, Wright often added to the pattern by using glass stops that extended past the frame. This is called a reveal. The family lore within the Beachy line is that Mrs. Beachy did not want art-glass windows. She got wood.

Dining room, Frederick F. Tomek House, 1907, Riverside, Illinois. The ceiling laylight is rather plain. It uses the same type of line as the Bradley House seven years earlier. There is little attempt to relate it to adjacent ceiling panels or to the windows.

Wright seemingly began to go beyond the expressed wishes of his clients, injecting more art into the work. One feature was that he began to use their initials as part, or all, of the pattern. Were these subjects requested by the client, or was Wright expanding his repertoire, or had he challenged himself to be creative with initials? One ceiling panel even included a profile of the front elevation of the house.

This nonsymmetrical way of designing indicated that Wright was forgoing the use of plants for his abstractions and moving toward nonrepresentational designs, just pure pattern.

Above: Dining room, Frederick F. Tomek House, 1907, Riverside, Illinois. Three units of the ceiling laylight are set between the two longitudinal beams. Each laylight unit looks like the others, but their design is unrelated to the windows.

95

Entry window, Laura Gale House, 1909, Oak Park, Illinois. This is one of Wright's earliest asymmetrical designs. The top-heavy pattern and bottom band relate this design to the Tomek House.

Living room window, Glassner House, 1905, Glencoe, Illinois

Left: At first look, this pattern appears to be based on that used at the Darwin D. Martin House (see p. 86) of just a few years prior, but it is simplified in that the Martin checkerboard becomes a series of squares in the Glassner House and the bold bottom square is now a simple square at the juncture. The design continues the multiple-border technique used by Wright nearly all the years he designed lightscreens. Again, the "tree of life" motif does not apply, as there are fourteen branches instead of the traditional twelve. The materials are the flat zinc came with some of the most beautiful iridescent glass in any Wright building.

Billiard room door,
Frederick C. Robie House,
1909, Chicago, Illinois. The
pattern is located at the top of
the door. There is very little
came work and no colored or
iridescent glass at the bottom.
In many ways, the design is
based on those first used at the
Willits and Thomas Houses,
with medallions at the upper
sides of each unit. The zinc
cames are flat bar rather than
the colonial profile that Wright
so often used. The cames are
all the same width throughout
the pattern.

Arthur Heurtley House, 1902, Oak Park, Illinois.

Right: The dining room windows are among the simplest of all Wright's lightscreens using metal came and gold mirror glass, a delicate version of those in the W. E. Martin House. The use of the gold glass in the Heurtley House is also similar to its Forest Avenue neighbor, the Thomas House.

Below: Behind the pair of living room ceiling laylights in the cathedral ceiling are a series of incandescent lights set into a wood box in the attic space above the living room. The design is defined by fine colonial came work that employs triangles in much the same way as in the Dana House, particularly in the hanging lights in the dining room. The pattern is an abstraction of the profile of the house (left), inverted in the screen. The green, brown, and gold seen in the glass were also the colors of the original walls.

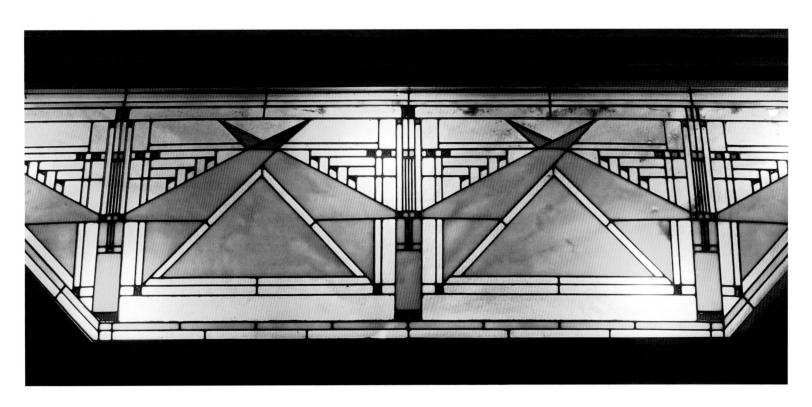

CHAPTER 7

Developments in Abstraction

After Wright's hiatus with Mrs. Cheney in Europe in 1909–10, his art-glass patterns and approach matured. His designs from 1910 to 1925 are not always considered among his finest, but they are some of the most abstract. They parallel and in many ways precede similar advances in the field of abstract painting.

Wright's general output dramatically decreased in this period, but his creations were larger in scale and there were many distractions in his personal life. He had left his family and taken up housekeeping with the wife of a former client. She and her children, along with several employees, were murdered and Taliesin was burned in a fire. He became involved with another woman, was finally granted a divorce from his first wife, married the third woman, divorced her, and married a fourth. His mother died. His mentor, Louis Sullivan, died, and Wright spent years out of the country, while in the U.S., Taliesin burned a second time. All of this in less than twenty years. Is it any wonder that he might have had difficulty concentrating on work?

Facing: Master-bedroom windows, Aline Barnsdall House, Hollyhock House, 1919, Los Angeles, California. The shadows from the floor-to-ceiling lightscreens in the master bedroom give the wall texture, as do also the leaves and branches just outside. The pattern appears to end before it reaches the top of the window, a technique Wright developed during this time.

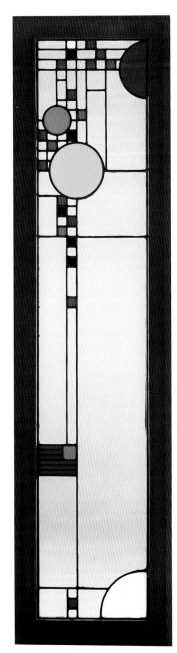

Window, Coonley Playhouse, 1912, Riverside, Illinois. This is the sidelight to the entry on the north side of the building. It is one of several on this house that contain abstractions of the American flag in the lower third.

Beginning with the Coonley Playhouse (1912) and its circles and squares, Wright hung onto the last vestiges of representation in this forward-looking window pattern, commonly described as confetti and balloons. While confetti had long been an item for celebrations, helium balloons were quite rare in the early years of the twentieth century. One would not expect to find the confetti-and-balloons theme in a serious edifice of learning. The kindergarten was apparently not considered to be such a place. Wright knew learning could be fun, and his client was part of the leading edge of educational theory at the time. One aspect that is often overlooked but of vital importance in this design is the line of checkerboard Wright continued through all of the clerestory windows of the main room. The decorative band at the top is balanced with a minor one at the bottom, almost like the major and minor keys in music, as Leonard Eaton has discussed.

This line of continuity keeping the same checkerboard pattern is found in the windows of the Imperial Hotel (1915), which really must be seen in their original context in order to follow it as a band.

The dynamic diagonals used in the Winter Garden windows of Midway Gardens (1914) were used again in some of the designs found in the Barnsdall Hollyhock House. Midway's triangles allow adjacent windows to have inverted patterns, adding dynamic options to Wright's normal squares and rectangles.

The Little House in Wayzata (1913), which was dismantled and moved to the Metropolitan Museum of Art in New York, contains more of these abstract patterns and continues the use of continuity through several window panels or lights. The design does not bear the import of others from this time, but it did receive careful study by, and a challenge to Wright from, the client—all documented by letters to change and improve the glass design.

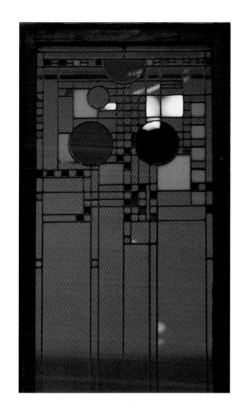

One of the triple windows, Coonley Playhouse. This is perhaps the finest series of abstract lightscreens Wright ever devised. The designs relate to each other but can also stand on their own individually.

Above: Clerestory windows, Coonley Playhouse. These two small series give an indication of not only the variety but also the continuity that connected the units down both sides of the clerestory in the central room.

Bedroom windows, Francis W. Little House, 1913, Wayzata, Minnesota. This bank of windows includes a pattern whose continuity crosses the window jambs. The awkward proportions are a result of several discussions, in person and through the mail, between the client and Wright. The balance of the upper pattern with the lower is unusual in that the break between the two occurs near the center rather than in the upper third of the design.

Winter Garden, 1914, Midway Gardens, Chicago, Illinois (demolished). One of the few designs that utilizes a long series of identical units. The asymmetry is especially interesting.

Wright's color choices of this era were not iridescent but flatter and more pure. He wrote in the July 1928 *Architectural Record* about this:

> I have used opalescent, opaque, white and gold in the geometrical groups of spots fixed in the clear glass. I have used, preferably, clear primary colors, like German flashed glass, to get decorative effects, believing the clear emphasis of the primitive color interferes less with the function of the window and adds a higher architectural note to the effect of the light itself. The kinder-symphony in the windows in the Coonley play-house is a case in point.

Wright also included only gold at the Imperial Hotel, purple at the Barnsdall Hollyhock House, red and white at the Midway Gardens, and white at the Little House of Wayzata.

The lightscreens from this period break up large expanses of glass and bring down the scale of the buildings. As Wright stated in the same *Architectural Record*, "The pattern may be calculated with reference to the scale of the interior and the scheme of decoration given by, or kept by, the motif of the glass pattern." They give texture and a little color to what would otherwise be large sheets of reflected light and give a hollow look to the buildings. Most of the lightscreen designs are created in lines and a good number extend the pattern into adjacent panels. Many of the openings where these lightscreens are set are deep, placing the window in a different plane than the wall surface.

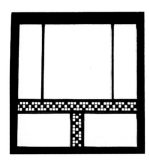

Reconstructed facade, Imperial Hotel, 1915, Tokyo, Japan. Ribbons of gold checkerboard glass originally ran through windows all along this level throughout the large building. The gold reflected the light of this tight site and enlivened the static design by adding the fourth dimension—dynamic time. Window unit above.

Bedroom sun trap, Aline Barnsdall House, Hollyhock House, 1917, Los Angeles, California.

CHAPTER 8

Concrete Lightscreens

Patterned concrete panels first appeared in Frank Lloyd Wright's work at the 1912 Midway Gardens; however, these were not pierced through. A few years later, Wright created openings between concrete panels of the German Warehouse (1916). Both of these buildings employed traditional masonry construction methods.

But in the 1920s, Frank Lloyd Wright threw out the traditional in his work and started with a clean sheet of paper. The structural, or construction, system for the Millard (1923), Freeman (1924), and Storer (1923; see p. 8) houses was unlike anything he had done before. He used neither frame-construction nor standard brick-construction methods. He invented a system of sixteen-inch-square concrete blocks that were to be stacked one on top of the other, held together by a grid of steel rods set into the joints.

Exterior, Alice Millard House, 1923, Pasadena, California. Casement windows are set into the inner wall behind the pierced concrete blocks. When viewed in full sun, the pattern overrides the pierced effect.

Wright placed plain-faced blocks in many areas of these houses but also designed intricate, three-dimensional patterns for the faces. At designated locations, the blocks were pierced all the way through. Some of these were backed by fixed plate glass, some were fitted with casement or sliding windows behind, and others acted as grilles for light from incandescent bulbs.

The pierced blocks occurred either singly or in groups, with some being widely spaced into patterns themselves. In these few buildings, Wright fully explored most, if not all, of the possibilities of concrete.

Opposite: Alice Millard House, master bedroom interior, 1923, Pasadena, California. These casement windows are set into the wall. There are two opposing sets of blocks for the walls of every California block house: an inner and an outer. The chandelier was a temporary installation and not a Wright design.

Below: Alice Millard master bedroom exterior.

CHAPTER 9

Ennis House,
Last of the Art Glass

There are few, if any, company records of art-glass designs or installations other than the Ennis House (1925). Most of what is known about his earlier work comes from brochures and published advertisements. While Charles and Mabel Ennis are not well-known personalities and did not leave a wealth of letters or other personal papers to know their direction given to Frank Lloyd Wright in the designing of their house, luckily, the building is in good condition and yields much information on its own. In addition, The Judson Studios of Los Angeles has records on the Ennis House, and one would expect that there would not be any question as to the attribution of design and construction of the glass. Nevertheless, some confusion exists.

As the building exists now, there are four different sets of window lightscreen patterns. These might be described as the desert series, the diagonal series, the purple squares, and the Des Moines group. All of the windows are set into wood frames; many can be opened and some are fixed.

Living room doors, Charles Ennis House, 1925, Los Angeles, California. These doors, sidelights, and transoms are a part of the ensemble that Wright first designed for the house as part of the desert series. They now exist only in the south elevations of the house. All of these lightscreens are fixed sash.

Living room window, Charles Ennis House. No photos have been located of the interiors during the time the Ennises occupied the house.

The desert series was probably designed by Wright. They appear to be abstractions of desert plants characterized by long, thin stems and feathery branches or leaves. (Wright considered Los Angeles to be the desert that it was rather than the lush, subtropical jungle it has become.) These windows are largely located in the south walls of the living and dining rooms. Very small cathedral-glass accents in a series of greens vary in value across a narrow range in small steps from top to bottom. These designs also use two came widths.

The diagonal series is closely related to the desert series but does not have its design sophistication. The horizontal subdivisions—in this case, six equal ones—occur regularly across the width. There are blue colors at the top and blue next to yellow at the bottom in every case. This group is largely in the north walls of the living and dining room and may have also been in the north wall of Mrs. Ennis's room, now used as the library, off the living room. The same pattern is used in two windows; though the windows are the same height, they are more than twenty inches different in width. The diagonals are set at much steeper angles in the narrower window.

Living room upper windows, Ennis House, north side. These are examples of the diagonal series. The tall window on the right is identical in size and is a continuation of the rhythm of the window openings on the facing page, right. It is the twin of one that is owned by a Pasadena collector, but there are none missing from the building.

The purple squares are located in Mrs. Ennis's room and the adjoining bathroom. They may have replaced, in part, some of the diagonal series in the upper wall of the room. The colors are contained within the vertical lines in much the same manner as in the diagonal series.

The Des Moines series is in the east wall as well as the door to Mrs. Ennis's room. These are near duplicates of designs by architect Arthur Heun of Chicago for a 1907 house for Mr. Brinsmaid of Des Moines, Iowa. The pattern was illustrated in the Giannini & Hilgart catalog, a copy

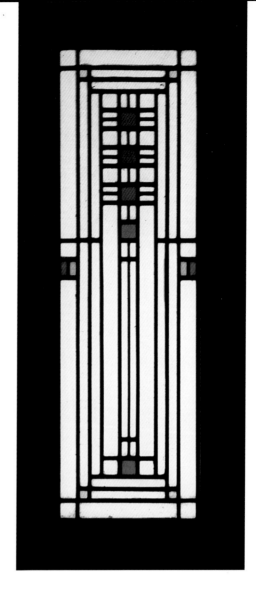

Above: Charles Ennis House, 1925, Los Angeles, California. The library windows align with and are in the same rhythm as some of the diagonal series in the north wall of the living room. There is some evidence, though inconclusive, that one of these diagonal series units was replaced at an unknown date by a window from the purple series. The evidence? A diagonal unit from the house that is held in a Pasadena collection has pits on what was the outside face, which means that it resided in the house for some amount of time and that it was replaced by something.

Left: This door from the bathroom to Mrs. Ennis's room is an example of the purple series.

113

West wall of Mrs. Ennis's room (now the library). This pattern is nearly identical to that designed by Arthur Heun in 1907 for the Brinsmaid House in Des Moines, Iowa, and illustrated on page 123 in the Giannini & Hilgart catalog. The slit window to the right is a simplified version of the larger example. How or when these alternate patterns were installed in the Ennis House remains a mystery.

of which is in the library at The Judson Studios.

Some confusion arises over one of the small diagonal windows being in the collection of an important Pasadena collector. There is a full set of these in the Ennis living room; none are missing. They are the same size as the purple-square set in the north wall of Mrs. Ennis's room. It appears that the diagonal design originally extended into Mrs. Ennis's room but was removed. The collector's example is finished with the same copper wash over the zinc came as the Ennis window, and there is some pitting on the exterior side of the piece. It is an obvious conclusion from the weathering that this piece was once installed in the Ennis House. When and why it was removed cannot be determined. The fact that there is a separate Judson quote for Mrs. Ennis's room leads one to think that the change occurred after the full sets of original Wright designs were installed. This would seem logical, except that the quote preceded the quote for the remainder of the Ennis windows. Judging from the length of time it would take for pitting to occur, replacement windows, therefore, must have been installed between 1935 and 1950, evidenced by the nearly identical weathering on all the windows currently in the house.

Of course, typical of all art and stained-glass windows throughout the U.S., none of the windows have any kind of identifying marks on them. Research would be facilitated if glass studios adhered to Claude Monet's maxim, It's not art until it's signed and dated.

Frank Lloyd Wright and The Judson Studios

BY DAVID D. JUDSON

(The Judson Studios of Los Angeles was founded in 1897 by the former painter
William Lees Judson and has been in continuous operation by family members since.)

The first noted acknowledgement of F. L. Wright in The Judson Studios records was posted on April 4, 1920. The entry is a reminder to see a Mr. Wright from the Chicago area about art glass. Nearly a month later a quote is given to the architect for the "A. Barnsdall Residence of Hollywood" at the cost of $2,025 and $40 for the garage.

Remaining entries regarding the Barnsdall job come in July, noting tile colors (most likely for the fireplace) to be shown to Wright, and in August Wright is sent tile samples and prices. Early in January 1921 there are revised set plans for Wright, though it is unclear whether these plans are for art glass or for the tile work. On January 28 more prices for the Barnsdall residence are quoted to Wright for art glass, which is listed as sold on May 24 for $3,060. The fireplace tile is billed on July 17 at $350 for time and material for setting.

The prices for individual rooms in the Barnsdall are listed on July 30, 1921. The following rooms were noted for art glass: owners, child's, nurse, pergola, music, child, dining, and sun. Listed next to these prices is "Sold with changes $1,400, mirrors $120." These two sold entries ($3,060 on May 24 and $1,400 on July 30, 1921) suggest that some windows were installed in the house at the end of May and the remaining windows two months later, in July. This entry on July 30 lists Schindler—instead of Wright—with whom the studio must have been dealing at the time. Schindler was believed to have overseen much of the Hollyhock construction while Wright was working in Japan. The Judson Studios would work again with Schindler at the end of 1928, constructing light shades for a house on Dundee Place in Los Angeles.

Further correspondence regarding the Barnsdall job is found in a photocopy of a letter written by F. L. Wright's office. The letter, dated April 21, 1921, is addressed to Weldon and Glasson of San Diego, asking that the window sashes they were constructing be sent to The Judson Studios.

The next entry for Wright comes on February 1, 1922. This note lists prices for 15 lanterns and 29 lights; whether they were ever fabricated is unknown. No records indicate that the lanterns or lights were ever sold, though this entry could represent the actual sale.

Later collaboration of Judson Studios and Wright is found in a contract for Mr. C. W.

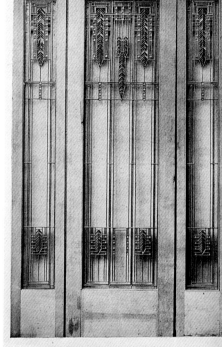

Doors for Brinsmaid House, designed by Arthur Heun, 1907, Des Moines, Iowa, from Giannini & Hilgart brochure, no date. This may have been the source for the design of the Des Moines lightscreens used in Mrs. Ennis's room, which has a nearly identical pattern. The Ennis originals are now in the collection of the American Wing, Metropolitan Museum of Art, New York.

Ennis dated May 11, 1925. The contract lists 10 windows to be fabricated for the house according to the details and colors approved by Mr. Ennis. Nearly two months later, on July 1, an invoice is drawn up for Mrs. Ennis's room, 1 glass mosaic, 6 windows for the dining room, 10 windows for the living room, and 2 windows for the closet. The designs for the windows at the Ennis House are much debated, and it is believed that some windows have been removed over the years and others added.

The mosaic over the fireplace also raises questions regarding who the actual designer and manufacturer were. While the invoice notes that Judson billed Ennis for the mosaic, it is unknown if Judson Studios manufactured the piece or bought it from Giannini & Hilgart, a Chicago-based company that had done many mosaics and stained-glass windows for Wright, and then resold it to Ennis.

There is an original Giannini & Hilgart catalog (not dated) at The Judson Studios containing a mosaic of essentially the same design—a wisteria with its trunk wrapping up the left-hand side, with the blue flowers hanging down across the top of the piece. Similar fireplace surrounds with this same wisteria exist throughout the country, three of which are known to exist in southern California, and appear to be crafted of the same technique. Did Giannini & Hilgart ship these mosaics across the country? We simply do not know. It is possible that Judson had some collaboration with Giannini after he moved to La Jolla, California, in 1906. The Judson Studios was heavily involved in

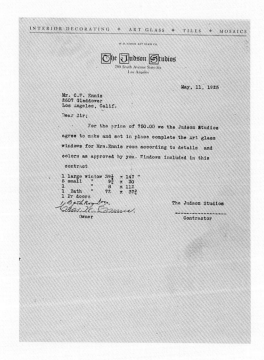

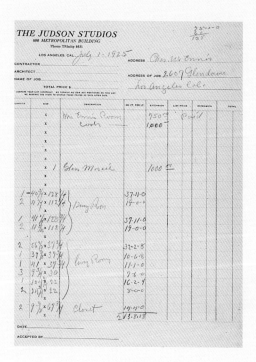

mosaic work during this period in southern California. It is possible that he shared the technique with the studio, or perhaps the client selected the design from the catalog. To this date it is unclear who designed the mosaics and where some of them may have been manufactured.

The Ennis House fireplace mosaic is not the only wisteria attributed to The Judson Studios. A second fireplace surround was discovered in early 1999, after it had been sold to another party. According to the family that originally owned the mosaic, Judson Studios installed this particular surround in a 1913 house on Lafayette Park Place in Los Angeles. The Judson Studios has not been able to find records of this installation. Interestingly enough, this piece was installed more than ten years before the Ennis House mosaic.

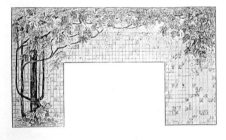

Plate from Giannini & Hilgart catalog, no date (circa 1906). This is one of a long series of wisteria-patterned fireplace surrounds. The origins of the design remain unclear.

Mosaic fireplace surround, 1914, Highland Park, Los Angeles, California.

117

CHAPTER 10

Tubes and Panels

One might not consider an aging architect to be at the forefront of innovative use of technology, but, in many regards, Wright was an exception. In 1936, at age seventy, he designed the Racine, Wisconsin, Administration Building for Herbert Johnson, president of the family business, Johnson Wax Company.

Johnson made known several considerations as he engaged Wright for his building. Because he felt strongly about encouraging his employees to make the most of their efforts, he suggested to Wright that he did not want the building to have standard windows that might allow his employees to be distracted or tempted to gaze out the windows. He did want the benefit of daylight and understood the problems with glare in a modern office. He also knew that controlling the humidity and temperature in the offices was critical, especially since the weather along Lake Michigan can change quickly. He considered that open windows would allow dust and dirt into the interior that could gum-up the delicate machines that were becoming more common in the modern 1930s offices.

Facing: Executive-office floor, Johnson Wax Building, 1936, Racine, Wisconsin. These Pyrex tubes are used in the interior and the exterior as walls and partitions. The radiused corners of these offices add to the visual streamline, and here the joints of the individual tubes are artistically arranged and mitered. They obscure the figures on the opposite side, cutting down on workers' distractions.

Seminar Buildings, 1940, Florida Southern College, Lakeland, Florida. Set into the little dark squares in the ends of the panels are small pieces of cutlet glass, or church glass. Each piece is a different color. This does not affect light received on the interior because the sun does not hit each small piece.

Living room, Taliesin West, 1938, Scottsdale, Arizona. The living room, as well as the drafting room, once had a more rustic appearance. The ceiling was white canvas, which allowed much more of the bright sun into the room than does the existing fiberglass ceiling material.

Johnson charged Wright with devising a scheme that would solve all of these problems. Wright had had experience solving most of them in his design for the 1904 Larkin Building nearly thirty years earlier. All the problems had been solved there except for the large plate-glass windows. Wright began his design for Johnson with lightscreens that would turn the corner between the wall and the roof, but being familiar with Luxfer Prism Company's products, as the design developed, he found another solution: he proposed the use of Pyrex tubes as manufactured by the Corning Glass Company of New York. The glass tubes certainly fit into the streamline aesthetic of the times.

Wright, as one might expect, saw the art in the arrangement of the glass tubes. He introduced tubes of varying sizes placed tangent to each other. They were wired to an aluminum frame for proper alignment and support, but they could be made only to certain lengths and had to have occasional joints and interruptions. He accomplished this in an ingenious artful manner—staggering the joints and curving the beginnings and endings of the run of tubes.

The tubes allowed daylight to enter the spaces to the degree that one could easily discern the weather conditions but not individual clouds or other features. The tubes also contain an air space that helps the insulating conditions at the openings. The one problem he was not immediately able to solve, however, was the seal between the individual tubes. The contractor installed grey putty, which dried, shrank and leaked. It was not until silicone caulk was developed that the leaking was satisfactorily resolved.

Wright explored other means of lighting interiors without the use of common windows and plate glass. In two buildings built twenty years apart, he solved the problem with translucent roofs. Taliesin West (1938) had simple canvas for the roof of its drafting room. The canvas provided shade and allowed filtered, diffused, non-glare light into the room, although it sometimes proved to be too much light in the Arizona desert sun.

A similar but more permanent lightscreen was employed in the Beth Sholom synagogue of suburban Philadelphia in 1957. Wright devised a double level of corrugated fiberglass panels for the roof as well as the walls. Again, he introduced pattern to what could have been a boring installation. At third points in the roof/walls, he designed structural supports that are highlighted by unusual details.

Wright also designed a dome of translucent rubber fabric for a series of houses for U.S. Rubber Company of Indiana in 1956, but they were never constructed. This same material, stretched over metal bents that are still in place, was originally used for his performance theater at Taliesin West. The fabric has more recently been replaced by translucent fiberglass-insulated panels.

Wright developed a system for turning entire walls into lightscreens and was not constrained by the limitations of window holes in walls. These explorations give a unique focus and character to the buildings that use them.

Beth Sholom Synagogue, 1954, Elkins Park, Pennsylvania.

Sanctuary interior.
The luminous roof is handled in much the same manner as was the original at Taliesin West, but it is made of more durable materials.

Sanctuary exterior.
The translucent roof panels appear more solid when viewed from the exterior than from the interior. The roof's subdivisions constitute one of the most stable arrangements possible.

121

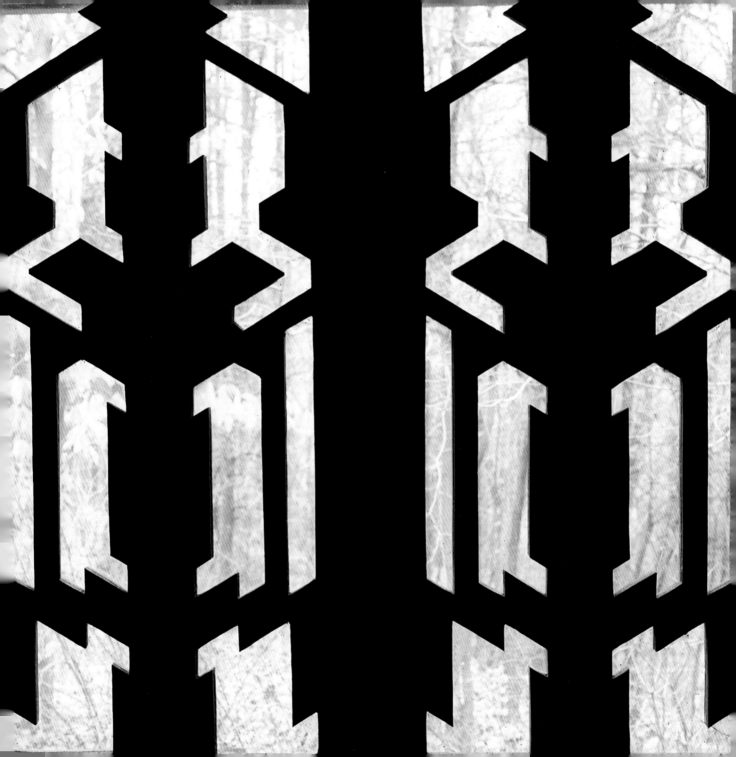

CHAPTER 11

Return to Wood

Wright certainly made an amazing number of design and technological advances during his seventy-year career. If the Winslow House or the Blossom House were compared with Fallingwater or the Jacobs House, no one could imagine that all these various buildings could have come from the same source.

One would find it difficult to imagine that anything that Wright did in the early part of his career would be re-introduced at the end of it. As with most of his output, the terms "always" and "never" are difficult to apply to any of his work. Wright started his career with Sullivan, designing wood lightscreens with cutouts in them. At the end of his career, he was doing it again.

For his later work of the Usonian era (1936–1959) Wright designed unusually constructed walls consisting of a plywood core with boards screwed to both sides. The windows were located along the edges of the sides and tops of these and the walls built of brick and stone as well. They were set into lines and groups. Most of these windows were fixed and did not open. Others were hinged at the top or side to allow the breezes in and out of the building. Wright not only added interest to the windows themselves, but the patterns he used in the openings created moving patterns as the sun arched across the sky each day. It was a moving display that

Facing: Bedroom windows, Pope-Leighy House, 1939, Woodlawn Plantation, Mount Vernon, Virginia. This pattern is a double use of the same unit, book-matched in casement frames. For the sake of economics, Wright repeated these silhouettes in the living room clerestories, but there they are set at ninety degrees to those in the bedroom. Such reuse between the rooms occurred frequently in the Usonian era.

Cut-wood screen, Weltzheimer House, 1948, Oberlin, Ohio.

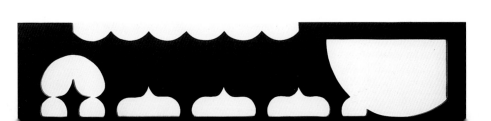

Facing:: Living room, Pope-Leighy House, 1939, Woodlawn Plantation, Mount Vernon, Virginia. Looking into the living room from the entry door, the vertical band of patterns is a small part of the larger design found in the clerestory band.

Living room-transom window, I. N. Hagan House, 1954, Ohiopyle, Pennsylvania. Each of these panels is set above the long built-in bench. The pattern is reversed, or book-matched, in adjacent panels. Some of these windows are hinged at the bottom on the inside and can be opened for ventilation.

also changed as the angle of the sun rose and fell from winter to summer and back.

Sometimes the lightscreen pattern would be taken from a portion of the plan or a landscape feature, but they were also just plain fantasy. Parts of the larger design would be used in repetitive vertical groups or as bookmatched windows.

Wright also continued to develop his concrete construction system and thought he had simplified it enough for the client to produce himself. He named it Usonian Automatic. No one who attempted this system could figure out what was supposed to be automatic. Wright introduced glass panels and blocks that were glazed in much the same way as the concrete-block houses of 1920s Los Angeles. Some were fixed and others opened.

An important design for lightscreens that has been little studied, though not perforated, was developed for the Price Tower. Each side of the building has a different arrangement of copper screens, grilles, and hoods, depending on the internal functions and the compass orientation.

Glazed concrete pier, William B. Tracy House, 1955, Normandy Park, Washington. The concrete, even when it is pierced, is structural and supports the roof of the Tracys' living room. The entire west wall is glazed with the pierced-block lightscreens and plate-glass doors, providing a spectacular view of Puget Sound.

Left: Toufik Kalil House, 1955, Manchester, New Hampshire. The blocks with darker borders are ventilation units that can be opened from the inside. Set in various strategic locations within the group, they provide maximum efficiency.

Below: South elevation, Gerald Tonkens House, 1955, Amberly Village, Ohio. Glazed blocks comprise the upper two-thirds of the walls in this Usonian Automatic concrete-block house, one of the longest of this style.

Price Tower, 1952, Bartlesville, Oklahoma. Every side of this square building receives the sun at different times of the day. Originally this was a combination apartment/office building. The offices benefitted from sunlight in the middle of the day, while the apartments benefitted in the morning and evening.

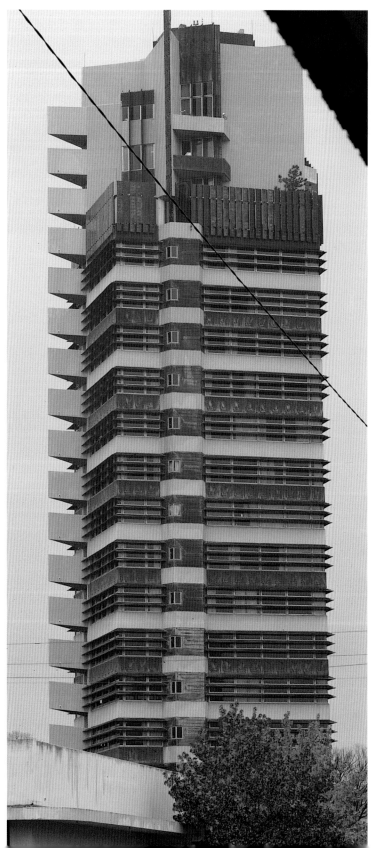

128

Index